THE DIVE

↓

Audrey and me setting the tandem record in Cabo San Lucas.

THE DIVE

ISBN   0-06-056416-4
REGAN BOOKS /

2004

A STORY OF LOVE AND OBSESSION

AUTHOR

↓ **Pipín Ferreras /** WORLD CHAMPION FREE DIVER

NATIONALITY	DOB	WORLD RECORD	LOCATION
Cuban	01/11–1962	561'/170 meters*	Cabo San Lucas

with Linda Robertson

1❸ Regan Books
Celebrating Ten Bestselling Years
An Imprint of HarperCollinsPublishers

Photography credits: p. ii, vi, viii, x, 96, Ron Everdij; p. 8, 10, 15, 28, Angelo Cordero; p. 18, 23, 26–27, 35, 60, 85, 122, 136, 208, 227, 228, 236, 237, 246, 277, Francisco "Pipín" Ferreras; p. 31, 44–45, 54, 74, 102–103, 116, 143, 168, 178–179, 194–195, 200, 204, 212, 220–221, 266–267, Robert Margaillan; p. 50–51, Carlos Serra; p. 64, 69, 106–107, 127, 128, 148, 149, 163, 184, 188, 189, 242, 260, Braase Gido; p. 79, 90, 273, Audrey Mestre; p. 277 courtesy of Swatch.

HarperCollins books may be purchased for educational, business, or sales promotional use. For information please write: Special Markets Department, HarperCollins Publishers Inc., 10 East 53rd Street, New York, NY 10022.

FIRST EDITION

Designed by Richard Ljoenes

Printed on acid-free paper

Library of Congress Cataloging-in-Publication Data has been applied for.

ISBN 0-06-056416-4

04 05 06 07 08 ❖/RRD 10 9 8 7 6 5 4 3 2 1

For Audrey

↓

CONTENTS

ACKNOWLEDGMENTS   ix

CHAPTER_ 01 /   Breathless   001

CHAPTER_ 02 /   Audrey   019

CHAPTER_ 03 /   Cuba   039

CHAPTER_ 04 /   The Wide Wide World of Sport   065

CHAPTER_ 05 /   Rapture of the Deep   097

CHAPTER_ 06 /   Pushing the Limits   129

CHAPTER_ 07 /   Blackout   169

CHAPTER_ 08 /   Unfathomable   213

CHAPTER_ 09 /   Burial at Sea   247

CHAPTER_ 10 /   A Tribute   261

< PHOTO: _ROBERT MARGAILLAN
DATE: _07/03.1998
LOCATION: _CAYMAN ISLANDS

ACKNOWLEDGMENTS

I have many people to thank for making this book possible.

First, of course, Audrey, who taught me the true meaning of love, and who showed me that the end of life as we know it is simply the beginning of another journey.

Thanks also to Anne Marie and Jean Pierre: your daughter gave me the happiest years of my life. I hope and trust I did the same for her.

My love and gratitude to my mother, Margarita, and to my two amazing children, Francisca and Luca.

A special thanks to Carolina Servigna, my assistant, partner, and truest friend: your unconditional support will never be forgotten.

My deepest gratitude to Carlos Serra, who offered me his friendship when I first arrived in the United States, and who stood by me like a brother: we had our differences, *hermano,* but I am truly glad we survived them.

A heartfelt hug to all the members of all the crews we ever assembled. Neither Audrey nor I would have made it without you. Thank you.

My utmost thanks to Mares. Without the constant support of the company and its employees, the development of our careers would have been even more difficult.

Thanks also to my dear departed friend Emilio "El Tigre" Azcarraga, who gave me a chance when I most needed it, and who introduced me to Mexico—the country where Audrey and I began our life together.

Thanks also to Judith Regan, my publisher; Bridie Clark, my editor; and to Linda Robertson, for the many hours she committed to the book. And, finally, a special thanks to Pablo Fenjves, who made it all happen.

↓

Chapter_ ONE:

BREATHLESS

Audrey during a practice dive in the Cayman Islands.

On the morning of October 12, 2002, shortly after dawn, I awoke from uneasy dreams and turned to look at my beautiful wife, Audrey Mestre, fast asleep on the unfamiliar bed next to me. Audrey and I had been together for almost seven years, and I was still filled with awe when I looked at her. She was too good for me; sometimes I felt as if I didn't deserve her.

I stood and made my way across the gray light of the hotel room and lifted the edge of the curtain. For the past two days, we had enjoyed perfect weather, but that was clearly over. I could hardly see the rising sun beyond the bruised, purple sky, and the trees along the shoreline were wailing in the wind.

I was not pleased. We had come to Bayahibe Beach, in the Dominican Republic, to set a new world record in free diving. No, not me: Audrey. I had been practicing the sport for more than two decades—diving to unimaginable depths without tanks—but she was a relative newcomer. Still, here we were to show the world that Audrey Mestre could beat the benchmark I had set two years earlier, when I had wrapped myself around a weighted sled, plunged 162 meters into the sea, inflated a balloon at the touch of a button, and rocketed back to the surface—all on a single breath of air. The entire trip—the distance of three football fields—had barely taken three minutes. But those three glorious, death-defying minutes are what it's all about. Those three minutes define me. Every time I reach the bottom and prepare for the long journey back, I think to myself, *Here I am, where I belong.*

I looked over at Audrey again, just now waking up. She smiled at me, yawned, and stretched her long limbs. *"¿Qué pasa?"* she asked.

"I don't like this weather," I said, frowning.

"Don't worry," she said. "It'll clear up."

That was Audrey for you: completely unflappable. In a matter of hours, she was going to try to set a world free-diving record, and she behaved as if she were looking forward to nothing more than a quiet stroll on the beach. That was part of her charm. There wasn't much that fazed Audrey. She took life as it came, and she treated every day like a gift. For Audrey, today was a day like any other. For me, her polar opposite, it was critically important. I had taught Audrey everything I knew about the sport. I had taught her how to survive at a water pressure that is eight hundred times denser than air; how to cram her lungs with oxygen while ridding them of carbon dioxide; how to coax her mind and body into a trancelike, energy-conserving state; and how to equalize her screaming ears at crushing depths. She had taken to the sport effortlessly, as if she had been born to it, and before long I realized she would soon surpass me.

She had another advantage: at twenty-eight, Audrey was twelve years my junior, and wholly undamaged by free diving. No blackouts, no crippling bouts of decompression, no close calls, no fear. But the biggest point in her favor was her unbeatable attitude. For Audrey, free diving was above all things a journey of self-discovery. For me, self-discovery was part of it, certainly, but I was also hooked on competition. I was the king of free diving. I was in the business of endorsing diving products, filming underwater documentaries, and setting world records.

And yes, I know: at that point, my last record was almost two years old. But that wasn't the issue. I wasn't there for me that day. I was there for Audrey. I was there to watch her turn herself into a star. I was there to watch my protégée become my successor.

"What are you thinking about?" she asked.

"I'm thinking about how beautiful you are," I said.

She got out of bed, moved toward me and gave me a kiss on the lips. "Relax," she said. "It's going to be great."

That was the other thing about Audrey. She always knew exactly what was going on in that hyperactive mind of mine, sometimes better than I knew it myself.

"I'm relaxed," I said. "Working on it, anyway."

But how could she expect me to relax? Our reputations would be riding on that sled with her.

We showered and dressed and Audrey decided to skip breakfast. She wanted to rest and get herself quietly centered. Beyond that, she wanted to avoid the press. Unlike me, she wasn't comfortable in front of the cameras.

"I should go see the guys," I said, kissing her. "I'll hurry back after breakfast."

I ran into a small knot of reporters near the lobby, all of whom were clearly disappointed that Audrey wasn't with me. One of them was this nerdy little Mexican who the previous day had come right out and asked Audrey, in my presence, what it was she saw in me. I had to laugh at his audacity, but I saw his point: a lot of people asked themselves that very question. I was a bald, outspoken, macho Cuban with a gift for pissing people off; she was a beautiful, auburn-haired goddess, and even greater beauty lay within. In some ways, Audrey seemed like a different species, leaps and bounds ahead of the rest of us on the evolutionary scale.

I wasn't always sure what she saw in me, either, to be honest, but I wasn't complaining. I waved at the reporters, flashing my gap-toothed smile, and went off to meet the guys. I found them in the dining room.

"Well, here's the beast. Where's beauty?"

That was Carlos Serra, my right-hand man, a bearded, garrulous Venezuelan who lived near us in Miami. He helped me with the logistics of each dive, which can be as complicated as surgery. A meticulous planner— some might call him anal-retentive—Carlos never left anything to chance. We often butted heads, but I needed him and we both knew it. My organizational skills left a lot to be desired.

Kim McCoy was seated next to him. Kim was our resident scientist, a short, always smiling oceanographer from San Diego who had led expeditions to the North and South poles. He was in charge of the computers, notably the one inside the two-foot cylinder that was strapped to the diver's back. The system allowed Kim to review the entire dive with pinpoint accuracy, second by heart-pounding second. Kim was a true Renaissance man. He spoke four languages fluently and knew as much about good wine and great opera as he did about the mysteries of the ocean. He was also the guy we turned to whenever things got crazy: our very own Spock, the voice of reason.

Pascal Bernabe, a schoolteacher from France, was seated next to Kim. Pascal was our most experienced safety diver, one of only a dozen men in the world who had crossed the 330-meter mark. He was always stationed at the bottom, at the point where the diver completed his descent and made his turn, a sort of Lifeguard of the Deep. At extreme depths, even oxygen becomes toxic, so Pascal was trained to breathe a special combination mix of gases, comprised of oxygen, nitrogen, and helium, called trimix. When he wasn't working with our crew, he could be found diving for red coral in Tunisia, looking for treasure on Mediterranean wrecks, or exploring the labyrinthine underwater caves in southern France.

Then there was Angelo Cordeno, our photographer, a Cuban from Miami, along with Orlando "Tata" Lanza, and Eduardo "Wiky" Orjuales, friends of mine from our youth in Cuba. Tata, slim and soft-spoken, was a professional spearfisherman in Mexico. Wiky, rotund and jovial—and quite clearly hungover this morning—had fled Cuba on a raft two years previously.

The last member of the team, as well as the oldest guy on the crew, was Matt Briseno of Hawaii. He was meddlesome, opinionated, and thought he could do everything better than the next guy—which wasn't far from the truth. Still, despite the quirks, everybody liked him, and things weren't the same when Matt wasn't around.

Missing, however, was one of our regulars, Cédric Darolles. Thin and baby-faced, with delicate, almost feminine features, Cédric was a superior scuba diver. We had met him five years earlier in Palma de Mallorca, Spain, where Audrey and I had been giving free-diving classes. Pascal Bernabe was there to help us, and Cédric had been his assistant. We thought the world of him. He was smart, funny, sweet, patient, and full of life, and we immediately asked him to become a member of our regular crew. From our first day in the water together, he held a special place in Audrey's heart, and she took to calling him her guardian angel. But now he was gone, having drowned a year earlier in a tragic cave-diving accident in Saint-Sauveur, France. Audrey flew to France for the funeral. She was the only one who had been able to soothe his grieving mother, but in many ways she was still grieving herself.

Cédric's absence notwithstanding, Audrey told me she was feeling confident that morning—perhaps more confident than usual. Her practice dives in the glassy waters off Bayahibe had gone like clockwork. She flew down and up the cable with such ease that I kept moving the target deeper. The crew was leery; Carlos and I argued about the change in plans. Yes, Audrey was making a substantial leap in a sport where progress was typically measured in one- to five-meter increments, and her previous personal best, which set a female record a year earlier in Fort Lauderdale, was 130 meters. And, yes, I was asking her to descend another forty-five meters, a full ten meters beyond the maximum depth recommended even for recreational scuba divers. But she was in a groove, in the zone, and both Audrey and I felt we should capitalize on it. Neither of us thought we were being reckless. We knew what Audrey was capable of, and we were looking forward to a stellar, record-setting dive.

Audrey would have been happy to have done it without all the international attention—without the reporters and the camera crews and the devoted fans. She wasn't about competition, or about setting records, or about seeing her name in the paper. In fact, when the cameras came out, Audrey tended to disappear. But this was one for the books—171 meters—and the aficionados had come out in droves.

We didn't talk much over breakfast, which is often the case on the day of a big dive. We all had our assigned roles, and we were lost in our own heads, reviewing and preparing for the day ahead.

When I got back to the room, Audrey was reading a book about Egypt. When it came to learning, she was insatiable.

"How are you feeling?" I asked her.

"Never better," she said.

I kissed both of her dark, regal eyebrows, her thin, long nose, and planted a final small kiss on her lips. "Get some rest," I said. "I'm going to get the boat ready."

It was drizzling lightly by the time I reached the lobby, but the wind had died down and I was feeling optimistic. The media were still waiting, and now included two cameramen from *National Geographic,* and news crews from PBS, Univision, Televisa, and Canal Plus. A team of documentary filmmakers was also present. I apologized for the delay, which had been brought on by the weather, but I assured them that the dive would go ahead as planned.

Then I hurried to the beach to help load our bulky equipment onto the eighty-five-foot catamaran that was to serve as our dive platform. We all remained a little tense. Conditions were less than ideal, we were behind schedule, and the length of the dive itself—the equivalent of a fifty-five-story building—was weighing on all our minds.

"Where's Wiky?" I said, feeling very much on edge. Wiky had been hitting the discos every night, staying up till all hours, and I didn't approve—particularly on the night before a big dive.

"He's on his way," Tata said, coming over to help me haul a tank on deck.

The amount of gear, as always, was staggering. Everywhere you looked there were hoses, gauges, tools, wet suits, weight belts, fins, masks, snorkels, and cameras. The bulkiest piece of equipment was the sled that Audrey would ride to her target. It was weighted down with a hundred pounds of lead, and it took three of us to get it onboard.

"Shit!" Matt cried out. "You almost smashed my fingers, *brodel!*"

At this point, Wiky showed up, still unshaven. He looked tired. I didn't like the shape he was in, and I made it clear. "Thanks for coming," I said with an edge. "Can you handle a two-hundred-ninety-five-foot dive?"

"Yeah, of course," he said. "I'm fine."

Tourists on the beach had gathered to watch us, some of them swaying to the loud merengue music that was blaring over the hotel loudspeakers. I wasn't in the mood for music, or for tourists. We finished

Audrey was doing fifty of these push-ups, five times a day, at the height of her training.

loading the boat and I saw that it was getting late. I told Carlos to bring Audrey out at 2 P.M., and off we went.

"Let's move!" I said. "*¡Vámonos!*"

As we motored out to the dive site, I noticed that the dark storm clouds were retreating and that the sea had ironed out to a slight chop. Okay. This was good. I could live with this.

I noticed Pascal checking the five tanks he'd be using on the dive, then turned to see Matt and Tata fiddling with the sled's decoupling pin. "I'll take care of that," I said. "You guys did it wrong the other day."

I went over every inch of the sled. I wasn't done checking it until we reached the site, some fifteen minutes later.

We dropped anchor and got to work rigging the sled. First, we put the lift bag in place, then we hoisted the whole unwieldy thing over the boom and swung it out over the port side of the catamaran, beyond the big pontoon. Tata and Matt helped me, along with two members of the boat's crew. Using the boom as a crane, we carefully got the sled into position and lowered it a few feet into the water.

Tata and I jumped in and swam over to make sure everything was good to go. I checked the lift bag first. I reached for the small yellow tank under it and gave the valve a quick twist, to test it. It hissed, puffing the lift bag, and I screwed the valve back down, nice and tight.

I looked over at Tata, treading water next to me, and he turned and hollered up to the boat. "The yellow tank—it's full?"

The answer came back: "Yes."

To this day, we don't know who answered. Our entire crew was up there, along with the crew of the catamaran, and the answer had come back loud and clear. *Yes.*

Just then, I noticed that a hinge on the housing of one of the video cameras was loose. It was leaking slightly. I called up for a screwdriver and a hose clamp and went to work on it, and when I looked through the viewfinder I discovered that the focus was off. Shit. I had to fix that, too.

Now the boats began to arrive, crowded with fans and curious tourists, and they kept coming: sponsors, resort employees, reporters, photographers, two paramedics, four lifeguards from the beach rescue squad.

Audrey arrived with Carlos at 2 P.M., while I was still in the water. She was uncomfortable with all the attention, but smiled gamely for the cameras.

I got out of the water and joined her and gave her a little kiss. "Everything good?" I asked.

"Yes," she said. "I'm anxious to get started."

"You look beautiful," I said.

She wanted to get out of the spotlight. "Let's get this show on the road," she said. "Tomorrow we can sleep in our own bed."

I went over to join Carlos. "Ready to put the line down?" he asked.

I nodded. We shoved the hundred-pound concrete disk at the bottom of the line into the water, then let out the cable and fed it through a pulley.

"Here comes one seventy," Carlos said. "And . . . one seventy-one."

Kim tied it off.

I looked toward the bow. Audrey was up there meditating, cloaking herself in serenity. Football teams like to get psyched up before a big game, working themselves into a crazed frenzy, but free divers do the exact opposite: they need to escape to that quiet place within. I returned to the water to finish fixing the camera. Unfortunately, it was taking longer than I'd anticipated, so I turned to Tata and told him to ask Audrey to start getting ready. He swam over to get her, and she slipped into her fins and lowered her body into the choppy seas.

The boats kept coming, jockeying for the best view, spewing smoke and blaring music. They were getting on my nerves. I rubbed my bald head furiously, an old habit, and signaled for them to please move back.

"*¡Poquito espacio!*" I hollered. "A little room!"

By this time, my safety divers were encased in black neoprene, hunched under the weight of their tanks. Pascal clung to the side of the boat, dwarfed by the five tanks he was carrying. He would be spending more than four hours underwater, decompressing, and he intended to pass the time by reading a soggy science fiction novel.

I finally finished fixing the camera and looked up at the leaden sky, which was now a faded denim hue, then turned as Audrey surfaced nearby. She had just completed a short, warm-up dive.

I swam over to join her. "You ready?" I asked.

"Yes."

"Let's do one more warm-up," I suggested.

We gulped air and dove down together, staying under for about three minutes.

When we surfaced, I again asked her how she felt.

"Great," she said.

She looked amazing. Calm, unflappable, glowing with good health. I, on the other hand, was a nervous wreck.

I kissed her.

"When you come back up, I'll kiss you again," I said. "Only it'll be different. You'll be in the history books with a new world record."

"Pucker up," she said, smiling. "I'll be right back."

We swam over to the sled and she lifted herself onto the crossbar.

"All good?" I asked.

She half-smiled, not answering, and turned her attention to the horizon, getting focused. Now she began to ventilate, inhaling and exhaling with mounting force, each breath deeper and more powerful than the preceding one.

Carlos called out: "Five minutes!"

Pascal and Wiky and our third safety diver disappeared into the water, to take up position. It was happening. We were on a strict timetable now. There was no turning back.

I watched Audrey as she neared the end of the countdown. She took one final, powerful breath—sucking every available particle of air into her abdomen, into her rib cage, into the upper lobes of her lungs, into her throat even—then looked across at me and nodded.

I pulled the release cord—once, twice, a third time—and the sled sank.

She was on her way into the deep dark blue, and I'd been down that same route so many times that I could feel exactly what she was feeling. The way her wet suit was becoming welded to her skin. The excruciating pain in her ears. The pull of the weighted sled as it propelled her toward the target. The 264 pounds of pressure pushing against every square inch of her flesh, compressing her lungs to the size of oranges. Her falling heart rate, by now slowed down to no more than twenty beats per minute.

At this point she'd be quizzing herself to avoid nitrogen narcosis. *What is my phone number? What is the capital of France? How old am I? Who's waiting for me up top?*

I was hanging on to the cable, treading water. Right about now, her body would be supersaturated with oxygen, and she'd be feeling energized and euphoric. I, on the other hand, was feeling anything but euphoric. I had been keeping track of the time in my head, and I feared she was moving too slowly. But just then, boom!—the cable jumped. I looked at my stopwatch: one minute and forty-two seconds. She had reached the bottom of the line a full fourteen seconds *ahead* of schedule. She had made better time than she'd managed on any of her practice runs.

I was ecstatic. I could imagine her down below, directly beneath me but 171 meters away, disconnecting herself from the sled and inflating the lift bag that would propel her back to the surface and into my arms.

I could imagine her shooting past Pascal, stationed mere yards away, ready to help in the unlikely event that something went wrong.

Carlos called out the time: "Two minutes!"

She was getting closer. In another sixty seconds she would burst though the water's shimmering surface like a dolphin, and I would swim to her side and take her in my arms.

I looked through my mask into the water, expecting to see the flurry of bubbles that would announce her approach. But I saw only shafts of light coming from above and behind me, trying to pierce the indigo gloom.

The seconds ticked by like hours.

Where the hell is she?

Three minutes—and still no Audrey.

I dove into the water and sped down to fifty feet, hoping for a glimpse of her yellow wet suit. But the line was empty and still. I swam back to the surface and looked at Tata. He shook his head worriedly; he was in the dark, too. We had no way to communicate with the safety divers below, no way to see or hear what was going on.

Three minutes and thirty seconds had passed since Audrey rocketed into the water. No free diver could descend to 171 meters and hold his or her breath for that length of time. She must have aborted the dive. Yes, that was it! She was probably buddy-breathing with one of the safety divers, and she couldn't come up because she needed to decompress.

A moment later, the lift bag bobbed to the surface. I felt a rush of blood to the walls of my throat. Something was wrong. Dead wrong. I had to go help. I yelled for the crew to hand me a tank.

Five minutes had elapsed. I went down to find my wife.

↓

Chapter_ TWO:

AUDREY

< PHOTO: _ROBERT MARGAILLAN
DATE: _07/03.1998
LOCATION: _CAYMAN ISLANDS

I met Audrey Mestre in 1996, in Cabo San Lucas, at the tip of the Baja Peninsula, where the Pacific Ocean meets the Sea of Cortez. It is a beautiful place. My favorite spot is a set of rocks known as Neptune's Finger, where a colony of sea lions makes its home. On the other side of the bay, there's a line of jagged peaks that poke out of the water like the spiky back of a sea serpent. Beyond that, and beyond the Arch, you can see a geological formation known as Land's End.

The town of Cabo itself, part honky-tonk tourist trap and part five-star resort destination, changed my life forever. I was there to bust my career wide open. My plan was to advance the No Limits world record to 130 meters, and I'd received $120,000 in sponsorship money, a portion of that from Emilio Azcarraga, the wealthy Mexican media mogul who owned Televisa, the network that would be covering the event.

Cabo is a hub of diving and sport fishing, but free diving had always been a mostly European phenomenon. The reason I was here, beyond the hope of setting a record, was to try to introduce the sport to the Western Hemisphere.

In the weeks leading up to the event, my crew and I were totally consumed by the logistics of the operation. We needed trucks, boats, dive equipment, cell phones, and walkie-talkies. We had to find a location in the bay that was deep enough to handle the dive. We needed to recruit local scuba professionals to serve as safety divers and cameramen.

I also had to spend hours in the water every day, day after day, preparing, mentally and physically, for the main event. And after every practice, after we'd made the necessary adjustments, stored the gear, checked and rechecked the gauges, hauled in the cables, and washed the tanks, we had to deal with the press. The sport was relatively new to most of them, and it was my job to answer their questions.

One evening, when I got done explaining the finer points of the sport to a pair of American reporters, I went off to join my crew at Margaritavilla, a bar near the marina. All the familiar faces were there, crowded around three tables, but there was one attractive woman I didn't recognize.

"Who's that?" I asked.

"She showed up in the hotel lobby this afternoon," Pepe Fernández told me. Pepe was my deepest safety diver in those days, a longtime friend from Cuba. "Charlie brought her over."

I looked over at Charlie Jones, the manager of Tio Water Sports, a rental outfit in Cabo. I don't know why I was so immediately curious about her, but I was. "She was asking about you," Charlie said.

"Me?"

"Yeah. She wanted to know if I knew Pipín Ferreras. She seemed very intent on tracking you down. Kind of cute, no?"

She *was* kind of cute, if a little on the skinny side, but I had other things on my mind. So I ate two burritos, had a slab of flan for dessert, and decided to call it a night.

"Hola."

I turned around. It was the mystery woman. "My name is Audrey," she said in flawless Spanish. "I wonder if I might ask you a couple of questions."

She had beautiful, brown eyes. "Sure," I said. "You a reporter?"

"No. I'm a student in La Paz in Baja California Sun."

Pepe interrupted to say that everyone was heading over to a karaoke bar, and we left the restaurant en masse and fell into step behind the crew.

"A student?"

"Yes," Audrey said. "I'm studying marine biology, and I've been reading about you. I'm curious about a couple of things."

"For example?"

"Well, I've been looking at the way the human body adapts at extreme depths," she said. "And I'm interested in blood shift."

Audrey was referring to the physiological changes that affect every free diver. The pressure is so intense that one's lungs threaten to collapse, and all of the blood in one's extremities rushes to the center of the body to keep this from happening. The lungs themselves shrink to the size of oranges, and actually fill with blood, and the heart gets pushed up and off to the side, tight against the chest cavity.

Audrey reached inside her bag for a pen and pad. "When, for example, you're at fourteen atmospheres of pressure," she said, "and all the organs in your chest cavity have shifted six or seven centimeters, can you try to describe exactly what you think is happening to your body?"

She seemed very knowledgeable. This was a far cry from the usual how-long-can-you-hold-your-breath-before-passing-out type questions.

"That's a tall order," I said. "Most of what I learned about blood shift I learned from Jacques Mayol."

"Oh, really?" she said. "There's a great free-diving tradition in France. Have you ever been diving there?"

"Well, no," I said. "I try to avoid France. I've had nothing but nightmarish experiences with the French. They're a very arrogant people."

"I'm sorry to hear you feel that way," she said.

"So you're from La Paz?" I said.

"No," Audrey said. "I'm French, actually. Your basic nightmare."

"I'm sorry," I said, mortified. "I was generalizing."

"No need to apologize," she said, smiling. "I think the French have pretty much earned that reputation."

We followed Pepe into the karaoke bar and tried to continue talking above the din. I asked Audrey about her research, and she said she'd been spending a lot of time in the lab lately, working with the lung of a cow.

"A free-diving cow?" I remarked. "This I must see."

She laughed, a sparkling, uninhibited laugh, and said something else that got lost in the noise of the bar.

"Do you want to go for a walk?" I shouted.

She nodded and followed me to the door and out into the street. It was blissfully quiet outside, comparatively speaking, but the town was still crowded with tequila-soaked tourists looking for a good time.

I turned in the direction of the beach and Audrey fell into step beside me. I wanted to hear her laugh again, but she was shy and a little on the serious side, and I could see I'd have to earn it. As we walked along, she kept prodding me with scientific questions—how much pressure did I think the human body could withstand, was alveolar gas a problem, had I suffered any notable side effects, particularly with my memory—and I found myself more and more intrigued by her.

"Did you know," she said, "that if you look at an X ray of a dolphin's pectoral fin, it has the same skeletal structure as the human hand?"

"I did know that," I said. "We all used to be fish. I still think I'm part fish."

"That's funny," she said. "When I was a little girl, I used to dream that I was a mermaid."

There was something magical about this woman. I needed to know everything about her. And by the time the sun came up, I had made a pretty good start.

Audrey was born on August 11, 1974, in Saint-Denis, France, a suburb north of Paris. When her parents brought her home from the hospital, her grandfather clapped his hands with delight. "Look at her feet!" he cried. "They're as big as flippers."

He was a diver. He saw the baby's distinctive feature as a sign that she would be one, too. Her grandmother quickly knitted a new, *larger* pair of woolen booties.

She was named Audrey by her parents, Anne Marie and Jean Pierre Mestre. It was an English name meaning "goddess of the water," and she showed an affinity for water very early on. For years, she was happiest in the bathtub, and she would remain there, splashing and gurgling, until her skin had withered like a prune. By age two, she was already swimming, and by four she was beating kids twice her age in local swim meets.

Audrey during a pensive moment.

"This girl is half-fish," her swim teacher told her parents. "Look at her. She can practically make it across the pool underwater."

During the summer, Audrey always traveled to the south of France, to spend a month with her grandparents in the seaside town of Palavas on the Golfe du Lion. Both sides of her family were born in Algeria, and they loved the ocean, which was clearly very much in Audrey's blood. Her parents were devoted scuba divers, and her maternal grandfather, Claude Rey Marechal, had been a champion spearfisherman in Algiers. Every morning, he and Audrey would walk hand in hand to the shore. He taught her how to breathe properly, so that she could take full advantage of the sport.

"When you inhale," he said, "you should feel your stomach pushing out. That means the air is filling every inch of available space."

By the time Audrey was five, she had her first wet suit, mask, snorkel, and fins, and whenever anyone offered to help her with the bulky equipment, she always replied with the phrase that would soon become an Audrey trademark: "I can do it myself."

When her grandfather went spearfishing, she tagged along, pushing herself until she could stay under almost as long as he could.

"The French have salt water in their veins," Audrey's grandfather used to say. And he wasn't far wrong. Diving had been popular in France since the 1920s. The early free divers called themselves "gogglers," after the goggles they wore, and they were something of a tourist attraction along the French Riviera, where people would gather to watch them harpoon fish. Frenchmen patented the first modern mask, as well as the first snorkel. Then Jacques Cousteau came along with his Self-Contained Underwater Breathing Apparatus (SCUBA), giving man a chance to go ever deeper into the mysterious ocean. There were still holdouts, of course, like Jacques Mayol, who loved the freedom of depending on his own lungs, and who went on to become one of the great heroes in the history of the sport.

When Audrey had grown strong enough to manage the rubber coils on a spearfishing gun, she received one of her own. But she never caught any fish; not a single one. She simply couldn't bear to hurt them. She loved them, and loved their world far more even than her own.

"Papa, you may think coral is just rock," she'd tell Jean Pierre, as if explaining something to a child. "But it is really a house for lots of living animals. At night, the teeny worms poke out and build more of their house. And then their skeletons become the reef."

She was lucky to have found her calling so early in life, but less lucky with her health. She had mononucleosis at age five, an appendix removed at six, and at seven she fell and broke her nose, which was thin and angular. She only cried when she was told that she wouldn't be permitted to swim for a few days.

At fourteen, the bad luck continued—she contracted typhoid fever and developed scoliosis, leaving her with a badly curved spine. For the next four years, she spent most of her waking hours trapped in a plastic corset, and her only release came during visits to the shore, when she removed the brace, slipped into the water, and was able to become herself again.

Water was the home she loved her entire life.

Later that year, when Audrey's father, an engineer, was told that he was being transferred to Mexico to work on a new water treatment plant in the capital, the first question out of Audrey's mouth was, "Is it near the water?"

Unfortunately, it wasn't. They were going to be living in the heart of Mexico City, the sprawling, noisy, congested capital, and they didn't go happily.

"No water," Audrey said. "How will I survive?"

Soon enough, however, their apprehensions lifted. They were won over by the Mexican people, their culture, even their weather. They wrote to their relatives about the bustling markets, the whooping mariachi bands, the Diego Rivera murals, and the haunting Frida Kahlo self-portraits. And they took excursions to the Aztec pyramids at Teotihuacán and Xochimilco.

The biggest eye-opener for Audrey, however, was her first weekend trip to Acapulco. The water in this country was warm and teeming with marine life, unlike anything she had even imagined. France was nice, certainly, but it didn't compare.

"It's an aquarium down there," she gushed to her parents. "The colors of the fish and corals are so vivid it looks like they've been painted."

Whenever they could, the Mestres drove to Tequesquitengo, a resort area near Mexico City, where Audrey could indulge her love of the water. The reefs were a whole new galaxy, populated by flamboyant, exotic aliens. She would lose herself in their mysteries for hours, reveling in the psychedelic splendor of this underwater world, exploring the coral pinnacles and sandy canyons, the sheer walls and the dark caves.

She loved all the movement and activity. Parrotfish pecking at the coral. A pair of clownfish cleaning their host anemones. A garden of eels studying Audrey from the safety of their burrows. She bought books on tropical fish and read about each species: goatfish, cowfish, scorpionfish, stoplight gobies, bluehead wrasses, golden hamlets.

One day, a shark cruised past, circled her, and went on its peaceful way. Audrey felt no fear; just pure, unadulterated awe.

Within a year, much to Audrey's chagrin, Jean Pierre Mestre was called back to France, his assignment complete. Audrey was happy to be reunited with her extended family, certainly, but she had left her heart in the waters of Mexico.

That same year, Audrey went to see the movie *Le Grand Bleu*. Directed by Frenchman Luc Besson, it was a portrait of the intense rivalry between the two most famous free divers in the world, Jacques Mayol and Enzo Maiorca. It was such a transcendent experience that she went back twice more and later bought the video. That Christmas, she asked her parents for only two things: tapes of Jacques Cousteau's underwater expeditions, and the book *Homo Delphinus,* by Jacques Mayol. In his book, Mayol suggested that human beings were part dolphin, and Audrey accepted this without question.

"I have decided on a profession," she told her parents a short time later. "I'm going to become a marine biologist."

Enjoying the breeze in Spain.

She was fourteen years old, and already knew exactly what she wanted to do with her life. And when her father came home a few weeks later, announcing that they were being transferred back to Mexico—well, for Audrey, it was nothing less than a sign.

During the last August Audrey spent with her grandparents in Palavas, she got herself certified as a scuba diver. This time, when she went back to Mexico, she intended to spend as much time as humanly possible exploring her beloved reefs.

For Audrey, the next two years in Mexico were nothing short of heavenly. The family took frequent trips to the coast, places like Ixtapa, where wild parakeets landed on their shoulders, or Puerto Angel, where Audrey saw her very first manta ray. At age seventeen, while vacationing in the Yucatán, Audrey went diving along the eastern side of the peninsula and found herself accosted by two playful dolphins. It was an experience she would never forget.

"I felt connected to them in ways I couldn't even begin to understand," she told me that night in Cabo, three years later. "You'll probably think it's corny, but there was something deeply spiritual about the experience."

I didn't think it was corny at all.

In the spring, the Mestres went to visit southern California and the American west, and Audrey fell in love with Seaworld. Sure, it was a big amusement park, but it was full of sea lions, sharks, dolphins, and orca whales. Her kind of people.

The family went to Hollywood, too, and to Las Vegas, and on up to Yosemite, but Audrey barely noticed any of these places. She was still thinking of Seaworld. She was thinking she could live in a place like that.

When the family returned to Mexico after their vacation, Audrey finished high school and began giving serious thought to her future. The family would be returning to France that summer, but she wasn't ready to go back. "I've fallen in love with the Pacific," she told her parents one night at dinner. "I want to stay in this part of the world."

There was a university in La Paz, in Baja California Sur, with a well-respected program in marine biology. Audrey wanted to have a look at it. Jean Pierre and Anne Marie were doubtful, but Audrey was their only child, and they didn't want to disappoint her.

The city was quite remote, though charming and very picturesque. It reminded Audrey's parents of Algeria. Audrey went diving, and swam with seals for the first time in her life. She returned from the water bubbling over with excitement. She had never seen such an abundance of fish. La Paz is on the east side of Baja, on the edge of the Sea of Cortez, which is a playground for whales, dolphins, sea lions, and seals, and it was clearly the place for Audrey. She was totally hooked. She even loved the name of the town: La Paz. Peace.

For the next two years, Audrey plunged into her studies and into the sea. She made frequent trips home, of course, but everyone could see that she was besotted with Mexico.

"Be careful," her grandfather joked. "You're turning into a mermaid."

"I would if I could," Audrey replied, grinning ear to ear. "I couldn't imagine a sweeter fate."

To hear Audrey tell it, La Paz was paradise on earth. The Sea of Cortez never failed to astonish her with its treasures, from the tiniest chameleon wrasse to a ninety-foot blue whale with a tongue as heavy as an elephant. And always there were the dolphins; those graceful, smiling, magical dolphins.

In her third year at La Paz, Audrey was required to write a thesis. She was very interested in mammals, particularly dolphins. She had never forgotten Mayol's suggestion that all people are part dolphin. She read everything she could about these playful, seemingly altruistic creatures. They always seemed to be smiling, and Audrey wondered if they knew something we didn't.

Her research took her all the way back to 600 B.C., to the works of Herodotus, who told the story of Arion, a palace musician who loved two things above all else: his lyre, and dolphins. One day, Arion sailed to

Sicily to compete in a music contest. He won first place and the judges sent him home with all the gold he could carry. On his way back to Corinth, however, the crew of the sailing ship stole his gold and ordered him to jump overboard. Arion asked if he could sing one last song, and the men allowed it, and before long his lilting tune had attracted a family of dolphins. At this point Arion flung himself into the water, and the dolphins saw him safely home.

There were dozens of stories like Arion's story, dating back through the ages, and to Audrey they all confirmed that there had to be some magical connection between man and the sea. We had come from the sea, she felt, and we still carried the sea within us.

Alas, academia was no place for magic, so Audrey turned her attention to science, specifically to the physiological changes that occur in mammals, and in men, at great depths. One of the more compelling changes is the so-called diving reflex, or blood shift. As one descends ever deeper into the water, the blood vessels in the extremities begin to constrict, shutting off blood—in humans, anyway—to the hands, feet, and eventually the arms and legs. At the deepest part of the dive, the only parts of the anatomy that have any blood flowing through them are the brain and the vital organs, and the flow has slowed to a mere trickle.

Audrey was riveted by her studies. She read the seminal works of Dr. John C. Lilly, *The Mind of the Dolphin: A Nonhuman Intelligence* and *Humans of the Sea*. She read about ultrasound experiments involving sea lions and dolphins. And she pored over the results of underwater radiology tests that showed how a free diver's lungs became simultaneously compressed and engorged, which seemed to confirm the blood shift theories.

"That's when I heard about you," she told me that night in Cabo.

I was immensely flattered that she even knew about me. Then again, in 1995 I had descended to 128 meters and set the No Limits world record in free diving, an event which garnered a fair bit of international attention. Audrey was interested in the sport, certainly, but she was more interested in the science. Her goal was to understand how the human body responded to pressure at those crushing depths.

Audrey struck a pose for me on the beach.

Other people before her had been curious about the same topic, of course, and Audrey had actually come across published studies that included references to me. Scientists at the University of Catania, in Sicily, noted my abnormally decreased heart rate and the severe constriction of my peripheral blood vessels. And there was an Italian professor at the University of Genoa, Massimo Ferrigno, who had turned me into his own personal lab rat during several days of tests. He measured my lung capacity, which was a good thirty percent larger than that of the average diver; noted that my Eustachian tubes were unusually straight, making them wonderfully efficient at equalizing the pressure in my ears; and said he was surprised at my ability to control my heart rate, which I did through simple breathing techniques—techniques I'd been practicing my entire life.

"When I found out you were in Cabo," Audrey said, "I decided to come and see you. But I didn't realize I was going to talk about *myself* all night. I'm sorry."

"I don't know why you're apologizing," I said. "I loved listening to you. And I could listen to you forever. But it's three o'clock in the morning, and I have a practice dive in a matter of hours."

"Now I feel *really* guilty," she said.

I laughed and walked her back to her hotel room, and when she opened the door I didn't feel like leaving her side. I suddenly had this crazy notion that I was going to spend the rest of my life with her.

"Can I spend the night?" I asked.

"No," she said, but she said it gently.

She reached for her key and opened the door and turned to face me. "Good night," she said.

"Please?" I whined.

She smiled, then reached up and kissed me, sending me on my way. "I'll see you tomorrow," she said. "Tomorrow it's your turn. Tomorrow I get to hear *your* story."

"It's a long story," I said. "I've lived a lot longer."

I was thirty-three. She was barely twenty-one.

"I've got plenty of time," she said, then disappeared into her room and shut the door.

I turned and made my way down the corridor. She was a maddeningly interesting woman, and this confused me a little. When it came to women, much as I hate to admit it, I had never been too good at seeing beyond the surface. But Audrey Mestre had magic in her soul, and I wanted to get to know her better.

"Pipín?"

I stopped walking and turned to find Audrey standing in front of the door to her hotel room, studying me.

"Okay," she said.

"Okay what?"

"Okay, you can spend the night."

I made my way back down the corridor.

"It's a long walk back to your room," she said, smiling shyly. "I figured you could use the extra sleep."

That was the night my life began.

↓

Chapter_ THREE:

CUBA

In Cabo San Lucas for the tribute dive. The tattoo
on my leg is taken from one of Audrey's drawings.

Over the course of the next three days, Audrey and I were inseparable. She moved into my hotel, accompanied me on all my practice dives, and spent every minute of every hour at my side. At night, after dinner, we would walk for hours along the beach, talking, getting to know each other, and we would always end the evening with a swim in the pitch-black, midnight waters.

The sea was our common home, and I felt that our connection went back a very long way—to a time that predated man's emergence from the water. I told Audrey that I had spent my entire life trying to reconnect with the dormant, aquatic being that lives deep inside us all. Before man crawled onto dry land, the ocean was his home—and part of me longs to go back to that place. Some people would have found such statements a little strange, but not Audrey.

"From the time I was a child," I told her, "I have felt more comfortable in the sea than on land. I swam before I walked. I could hold my breath underwater before I could talk. When I am in the water, I feel that I am truly home."

I had never before been so open with anyone in my life, but with Audrey I felt almost compelled to share every detail. I told her how clumsy I felt on land, and how graceful I felt in the whispering water.

Audrey understood this, and I loved her for it. She was my missing half; the woman I'd been searching for my entire life. When I looked at Audrey, I knew I would never be lonely again.

On February 28, 1996, only four days after I met Audrey, I did another practice dive. It went like clockwork. I took the sled down to 130 meters, inflated the lift bag, and rocketed back to the surface.

I climbed back onto the boat, kissed Audrey, and helped the crew pack up for the day. I was over by the stern with Pepe, hosing down the tanks, when he looked over at me and said in a furtive whisper, "What's wrong with you, *socio?*"

"Wrong?" I said. "I don't know what you mean. Nothing's wrong."

"You and the skinny French broad; I've never seen you like this before. What's going on?"

"I'm in love, *brodel. That's* what's going on."

Pepe reacted like he'd been slapped in the face. "You're messin' with me, right?"

"No," I said. "I'm not messing with you. She doesn't know this yet, but I'm going to marry that girl."

The last chore of the day was to hoist up the second, weighted stage of the sled, which was all the way at the bottom of the cable. Massimo Berttoni, an Italian living in Cabo, and a safety diver on this trip, had offered to take care of it. There wasn't much to the job. He had to swim down the line, attach a lift balloon to the sled, and return to the boat. But after several minutes passed, with no sign of Massimo, I began to worry.

"He should be back by now," I told Audrey.

I dove in and swam to about thirty meters but saw no sign of Massimo, so I returned to the surface, grabbed a tank, and plunged back into the water with the tank under my arm. At about 115 meters, I saw Massimo, tumbling toward the bottom, unconscious. I raced toward him and stopped his fall, then turned and made for the surface as fast as humanly possible. I knew it would have been prudent to stop to decompress, but at that point even a few seconds could mean the difference between life and death.

I broke through the surface, gasping, and called out to the crew. They took Massimo from my arms and laid him out on the deck. They tried to revive him with mouth-to-mouth and CPR, but they weren't getting a pulse. As Audrey hurried off to call for an ambulance, we laid Massimo on the back of a Jet Ski. Charlie took the controls and raced for the beach.

Before the shock had even registered, I started to feel intense pain in the joints of my left shoulder and my hips. It was the first sign of decompression sickness, otherwise known as the bends. I had ascended too fast, and the effect on the body is like uncorking a carbonated drink: the nitrogen bubbles were rebelling in my bones and in my veins.

I grabbed a tank and jumped back into the water, dropping to about thirty meters. When the pain finally dissipated, I slowly headed back to the surface, doing several decompression stops along the way. I reached the boat and looked up at several glum faces: Massimo hadn't made it. He'd been pronounced dead moments after he reached the hospital.

I was devastated. Massimo was an experienced diver. What had gone wrong? The police would later report his death as an accidental drowning, but they couldn't tell us why he had drowned, or how, so we would remain forever in the dark.

"You have to stop blaming yourself," Audrey told me. We were back in my room. I was lying on the bed, on my back, and she was sitting on the mattress, next to me. I had suspended training. I was thinking of calling off the dive.

"It's my crew," I said. "My dive. My show. I'm responsible."

"He was a professional," Audrey said. "I feel awful too but we all know that the sport is not without risk."

"So what should I do?"

"I'm not sure," she said. "But I think Massimo will be down there watching you and cheering you on. You wouldn't want to disappoint him, would you?"

I reached up and kissed her.

"I'm going to need another safety diver," I said. "How would you feel about taking his place?"

"Whatever you need," she said.

"What I need?" I repeated. "I'll tell you what I need. What I need is for you to come back to Miami with me after the dive."

She smiled, amused.

"I'm not kidding," I said.

"Come on?"

"I'm not. I've never been more serious about anything in my life."

Audrey didn't know how to respond. "I'm kind of in shock, to be honest. What about school? What about my parents?"

"School? Haven't you spent enough time with that diving cow?"

"It's a cow *lung*. Not a cow."

"And get your parents on the phone. We've known each other for four days. I think it's high time I met them."

The following day, we rented a car and headed for La Paz. Audrey had reached her parents in Mexico City and told them all about me, and all about Miami. They were concerned because Audrey sounded as if she had already made up her mind, and they asked us to meet them back at the university to talk it over. They probably figured this would give them a psychological advantage. If Audrey was that close to her school, a gentle push might get her through the door and back to class.

It was a three-hour ride through dusty, half-paved highways, dry riverbeds, and miles of cacti. "We're getting too far from the water," I said. "I hate being this far from the water."

"It's time to tell me your story," Audrey said.

She was right. It was. And that's exactly what I did.

I grew up with the sea as my backyard, in a big house on a cliff that overlooked Matanzas Bay, on the northern coast of Cuba. My mother, Margarita, was one of six children, born in extreme poverty, but at the age of two she was adopted by a kindhearted doctor who owned that big house on a cliff.

While she grew up in comfortable circumstances, she never forgot her roots, and in those prerevolution days her heart was with the poor people of the island nation. By the time she reached college, she had become a student radical, throwing her support behind a scruffy young lawyer named Fidel Castro. At around the same time, she fell in love with Salvador Ferreras, the leader of a political cell at the university in Matanzas. They got married, joined the revolution, and before long were smuggling weapons and supplies to the guerrillas in the Sierra Maestra.

When Castro swept to power on January 1, 1959, having overthrown the military dictator, Fulgencio Batista, my parents became part of his government. Three years later, on January 18, 1962, I came along. They called me Francisco, after Saint Francis, and while I was a big baby—a whopping eleven pounds—I turned out to be a sickly, asthmatic child.

Every day, my nanny, Haydee, would carry me down the rocky steps to the quiet little beach below, thinking the salt water would do me good. Those early dips in the ocean were the best part of my day, a harbinger of things to come.

My parents were preoccupied with their work, so they missed large parts of my early life. I was almost three years old before either of them noticed that I showed no inclination toward walking or talking.

"But look at him in the water!" Haydee told them. "In the water, he's as graceful as a fish."

By the time I was three and a half, I still wasn't walking, and still hadn't uttered my first word, and Haydee began to worry. She was a follower of Santeria, the Afro-Cuban religion, and she believed in Olokun, the god of the ocean. She would make an offering to this powerful deity and seek his blessing, and I would grow into a happy, healthy boy. One fateful night, in a candlelit clearing in the woods, and without the knowledge of my parents, a ninety-year-old Santero priest conducted a ceremony on my behalf. To the pounding of drums, people in white robes sacrificed goats, hens, pigeons, snakes, and frogs, determined to free the clumsy little mute from the evil spirits that possessed him.

There was music, chanting, blood, and prayer, and plenty of tears— mine!—but three weeks later I took my first step, and at home this was cause for celebration. I had a peculiar gait, to be sure—I stood on the balls of my feet and pointed my toes, as if I were in the water, kicking— but at least I was ambulatory.

The next goal was to get me to say something intelligible, and my father had me focus on the word *Papa*. For days on end, everyone concentrated on that one word, repeating it tirelessly, until one day I actually opened my mouth and squawked: "Pipín!" It was close enough. And it made a good nickname. So it stuck.

Once I became mobile, I could fully explore the lush jungle around our house, chasing its many inhabitants. For a kid, it was heaven. I ran after iguanas, peacocks, and our old bulldog, Champion. I climbed the banyan trees and fed the monkeys. I cooed at our canaries and they learned to coo right back.

Most of the time, however, I was drawn to the water. Matanzas Bay captivated me with its changing colors. It was silver one moment, emerald the next, and shimmering turquoise a moment later.

By the time I was eight, thanks to a friendly neighbor who'd been impressed by my aquatic skills, I was spearfishing. "Your son is part dolphin," the man told my parents. "I'm going to teach him how to use a spear gun. There will always be fresh fish in this house."

He was right. There was always fresh fish in our house, but my parents were seldom there to enjoy it. They were caught up in the fervor of building a new Cuba. My mother studied political science at the University of Havana and came home only on weekends, and even then she was too busy for me, doing volunteer work for the neighboring poor. And my father was a lawyer, on his way to becoming a judge. It seemed they were too busy for each other, too, and before long they grew apart and got divorced.

By the time I was ten, my extended family had been torn apart by Castro's policies, and half of them had fled to Miami. Not my parents, though. They would remain faithful to El Comandante until the bitter end. My mother enrolled me in a boarding school in Varadero. It was run by the sports ministry, and the goal was to churn out athletes by the dozens, as their counterparts were doing in the Soviet Union and East Germany. An Olympic gold medal was always good for morale, especially if it humbled any capitalists.

The school was housed in a huge mansion that had once belonged to a wealthy American businessman, and it sat near the edge of Cuba's most famous beach. It was horribly regimented, and I hated it. I particularly hated the fact that we were forced to memorize the teachings of Marx and Lenin, and to tirelessly pledge our allegiance to cause and country: "Onward pioneers! We will always aspire to be like Che!"

On weekends, I would escape to do what I loved most, spearfishing. My best friend, Tata Lanza, lived near the water, in Varadero, and he waited for me every Saturday. In Cuba, catching and selling fish was illegal, as was any form of private enterprise, but Tata and I ignored the law and turned our adventures into a very lucrative business. The close calls with the harbor police only added to the excitement.

One time we had a close call of another type. We were some twenty-five meters down, and I speared a hefty snapper, and returned to the surface with my prize. I expected Tata to pop up nearby, but he didn't do so. A full minute went by and I began to worry in earnest, but suddenly there he was, coming up for air and gasping like a beached guppy.

"Shit, *socio*! Didn't you see what happened?"

"No," I said. "What happened?"

"My leg got caught in some lousy fishing line. I almost drowned! Some friend you turned out to be!"

"Look at it this way, Tata," I said, grinning broadly. "According to my calculations, you were down there for almost three minutes. You're clearly in excellent physical shape, my friend."

When we weren't in the water, we'd go down the beach to watch Cuba's national spearfishing team at work. There were twelve of them, and they shared a house in Varadero. To me they were genuine heroes, bigger than any sports figure, bigger even than Cuban baseball slugger Antonio Muñoz. They had state-of-the-art pneumatic guns, American-made diving masks, and long-bladed fins. Man, what I could have done with that equipment!

One day, Tata and I heard about a spearfishing competition, and we got a chance to show the big boys what we were made of. There were thirty teams, with two men per team, and we were all ferried out to sea on the *Ferro Cemento,* a bulky Cuban-made freighter. We spent the night

With members of the team in Miami, just before we flew to the Dominican Republic.

on deck, in hammocks, and the next morning, bright and early, the competition began. The rules were simple: each team was given a rowboat and five hours. When the time was up, the team with the most fish won.

Tata and I were the youngest competitors, but we caught six hundred pounds of fish, winning the competition by a narrow margin.

"How far down can you go?" one of the men asked me.

"More than fifty meters," I said.

"Liar!"

"And I can hold my breath for four minutes!"

Back on dry land, I found myself being transferred to the Camilo Cienfuegos School, in Guanabo, near Havana, the next rung on the ladder to athletic glory. We were repeatedly told that El Comandante was providing for us and that in return he expected us to bring home plenty of gold medals. It was confusing. Castro had once condemned swimming as a bourgeois, country club sport, a *white* sport, but then he realized that an island nation ought to be able to produce a few record-breaking swimmers, and he began pouring funds into the effort.

By this time, my mother was working in the foreign relations ministry and my father had been made a judge in Matanzas. I saw my mother from time to time, but I rarely saw my father, and I resented them for it. I was jealous of their dedication, and I became a stubborn, rebellious kid. I didn't want to be a tool for Castro—in my mind, the man had taken my parents from me—and I began to slack off at school, both in my training and in my studies. I hated it. There was nothing more mind-numbing than swimming laps and staring at the black lines at the bottom of a pool.

By the time I was fifteen, I was regularly cutting practice to go spearfishing in Matanzas. I hung out along the Malecón, Havana's crescent-shaped seawall, with the rest of the fishermen, and I was learning to dive deeper and stay down longer than all of them. I was a competitive kid, and I really hated losing.

I forged a diving mask by melting rubber from Soviet boots around two ovals of glass. It leaked a lot, but it was better than nothing. My fins were also homemade, a pair of big old boxy things fashioned from hunks of plastic, and my spear was a metal rod, filched from a construction site and sharpened to a nubby point. That was the way things were done in Cuba. You to be *un vivo;* you had to live by your wits.

Havana's premier spearfisherman in those days was El Ronco, the Hoarse One, a compact, foulmouthed, combative little guy whose violent fights often landed him in jail. He had seen me fish, and one day he took me out to sea with him, as his helper. I watched from the sunface, trying to pick up a few pointers, but eventually I got tired of sitting on the sidelines and begged him to let me try his gun. He was amused, but he gave me a chance, and when I returned with a twenty-five-pound grouper his amusement gave way to contained amazement.

"That's not bad, kid," he said. "You have promise."

We returned to shore with two hundred pounds of fish, and El Ronco took all the credit. I kept my mouth shut—it wasn't worth getting beat up over a few lousy fish—and my discretion paid off. We became partners, a familiar sight along the shore. Old El Ronco and his young friend, Mini-Submarino.

I skipped school more and more frequently. I loved the water, but I loved it on my own terms, not on theirs. The hundred-meter breaststroke was as uninteresting to me as the confines of that overchlorinated pool. I longed for the open sea and the unexplored depths. I wondered if I could learn to breathe underwater. I'd done it once already, in my mother's womb, submerged in amniotic fluid. Maybe there was a trick to it. Maybe I could figure it out on my own.

Eventually, I lost all interest in school. Even under the best of circumstances, even if I really was as good as they said I was, what would it lead to? A gold medal meant less to me than an afternoon in the ocean. Plus I was sick and tired of being *Comrade* Ferreras, sick of being dragged off to the sugarcane fields to help with the harvest. The next time I was due to go to the fields, I stood my ground.

"I don't like harvesting sugarcane," I said. "I like fishing."

"*Comrade* Ferreras! This is your last warning."

"Okay by me."

I was expelled, of course. My parents were humiliated. They felt I had blown my one real chance at living the good life of a Cuban athlete. I, on the other hand, had different notions of the so-called good life. I went to work in the port city of Batabano, learning about boats, navigation, migration patterns, and the weather. Sometimes I'd be out at sea for weeks at a time, and I would think, *If I never see land again, I won't miss it.*

I worked at a sponge farm, for a lobsterman, for a shrimper. I got a job on the *Uaican,* a dive ship, helping government treasure hunters on salvage operations. I was almost eighteen and I'd never been happier in my life. A day didn't go by that I didn't learn something new about the sea.

But on my eighteenth birthday, things went to hell. I was tapped for mandatory military service, and I found myself living in a barracks, far from the water, landlocked and hopelessly lost. For three months, I endured it, and just as I was on the verge of defecting, I ran into an officer who had heard of me from the old days with El Ronco. He took me out spearfishing, and I showed him and his fellow officers how it was done. The officers caught plenty of fish, and they were happy, and treated me well. That too was part of my education. I had a small gift and it helped me forge unlikely friendships, friendships which helped me survive.

A year later, I left the army. My mother had long since remarried, and her husband, a captain in counterintelligence, helped me get a discharge. He was a terrific man, and he was always there for me, but I remained a little lost. I was no longer an athlete, I didn't intend to become a soldier, and I certainly wasn't an intellectual. I had a talent for holding my breath and swimming great distances under water, but—at the end of the day—what did that amount to?

I met a girl, Luisa, and she kept me busy and out of trouble. We moved in with my mother and her new husband, and tried to stay out of their way. Luisa had been kicked out of ballet school, and she was as disaffected as I was. We thought of ourselves as nonconformists and hung out with a crowd of equally aimless young Cubans. We considered ourselves to be rebels, the rebels who were rebelling against the original rebels. Our parents had embraced the ideals of the revolution, but we saw the *reality*, and it was grim.

There were no jobs. The infrastructure was collapsing. People were going hungry. Cuba had once been the third largest economic power in Latin America, but it had slipped badly and was slipping further still. Before long the government was handing out ration cards: the island was even running out of food.

Fortunately, the capitalist in me saw this as an opportunity. On an island full of hungry people, the spearfisherman was king. I tracked down El Ronco and resuscitated our old partnership. Early every morning, we'd hop on his rusty, Chinese-made bicycle and pedal to the beach. By midday we'd return weighed down with fish, which we sold on the black market. I was making eighty dollars a week, a fortune. I felt like a successful capitalist and it inspired me to ask Luisa to marry me. That seemed a little bourgeois for her taste, but it was worth a shot. And that's how I became a husband at age nineteen. I had accepted my lot in life. To be a husband and a fisherman and a breadwinner. It could have been worse. I was happy. I felt there was something heroic about going to work every day and putting food on the table.

El Ronco and I ventured in and out of hidden coves, far from prying eyes. One morning, as I was diving in the forbidden waters of Bahía Hondo, thirty meters down in an unspoiled bay teeming with huge fish, I heard an unusual, high-pitched whining noise directly behind me. I turned to investigate and found a Russian submarine bearing down on me, and watched, stunned, as it cruised past, the red star on the vessel's bow passing me at eye level. I was dangerously low on air by this time, so I shot to the surface.

"El Ronco!" I yelled, gasping as I broke through the surface. "There's a Russian sub under our asses!"

"You're crazy," he said, laughing. "You're narked."

I'd been drunk on nitrogen before—it's not unusual when you go beyond thirty meters—but that morning I was stone-cold sober.

"I'm telling you the truth, man! I could have reached out and touched it."

He never believed my story. And neither did Luisa. She was sick of my stories, anyway. All I ever talked about was the sea, and she didn't share my enthusiasm for it. She was bored with me and bored with the marriage.

In 1982, when I was twenty, an Italian magazine photographer arrived in Havana to take pictures of Cuba's magnificent reefs. When he asked the locals where he'd find the biggest fish, they told him to talk to me. He tracked me down and offered me twenty dollars to be his guide. I accepted fifty.

"My name is Vincenzo," he said.

"Mine is Pipín."

As it turned out, Vincenzo was an avid spearfisherman, and when he was done taking pictures we plunged in to have some fun. He had a hard time keeping up with me, and he was winded after a few dives. "Pipín," he said, struggling to catch his breath. "Have you ever heard of free diving?"

"Yes," I said. "Many, many years ago, Enzo Maiorca came here from Italy to do some diving. But I was just a kid. I really know nothing about it."

"It's very popular in Italy," he said. "And not just as a pastime, either. It's become a competitive sport."

That night, at the hotel, Vincenzo told me all about free diving. It went back to 3000 BC, he said, though of course they probably had another name for it, and he claimed there were Mesopotamian drawings and pottery decorations depicting free divers in action.

There had even been free divers in the time of Alexander the Great, he said, who used their talents to help scuttle opposing warships. And the Greeks had a famous free diver of their own, Glaucus, who was able to stay submerged for several minutes, thanks to a magical seaweed. "That's the story, anyway," he added with a shrug.

After Vincenzo went back to Italy, solemnly promising to stay in touch, I went to the library in Havana to read about free diving. I read about the pearl divers of the Persian Gulf, who would pierce their eardrums to relieve the pressure. And I read about the pearl divers in

Broome, on the western coast of Australia, who drowned by the dozens in their desperate search for the legendary *Pinctada Maxima,* the biggest pearl in the South Seas. Many Aborigines were kidnapped and forced to work in those treacherous waters, and those who didn't perform were left to the sharks. Things got so bad, in fact, that in 1875 the Australian government passed the Pearling Act, but it had little effect on the inhumane treatment of the divers, and they continued to die by the hundreds. All along the coast, pearls became known as "tears of the moon."

As I continued to pore through the books, I learned about freediving cultures that existed to that very day. The Bajau Laut of Malaysia had been harvesting shellfish for two thousand years. They were nomadic boat people who spent most of their lives at sea, and they even gave birth in the water.

Women divers—the Ama of Japan and the Jamsu of Jeju Island, south of the Korean peninsula—had been passing their skills on to their daughters for generations. The Ama, who dive for abalone, have a curious habit of whistling before submerging, which for a long time was thought to be part of a quaint tradition. But scientists eventually figured out that it was a form of preparation, physical and psychological, for the dive ahead. The Jamsu dive for sea urchins, conch, and seaweed, and they bring them up in basket buoys tied to their waists. Both of these cultures were dying out, unfortunately, and the few remaining practitioners were well into the fifties and sixties,

One of my favorite free-diving stories was about a Greek sponge diver, Stathis Hatzis, and dated back to July 1913. Apparently, the Italian navy vessel *Regina Margherita* was pulled loose from her anchor during a storm in the port of Karpathos, on the Aegean Sea. Crewmen tried to dive down and tie a line to the anchor, but at about eighty meters it was unreachable. After the first mate drowned in the attempt, the captain promised a large reward to the local sponge divers—known as *gymnos,* or naked divers—if they could recover the anchor.

Hatzis, a rickety man with a push-broom mustache, volunteered to do it. He claimed he could hold his breath for four minutes. The ship's doctor examined Hatzis, who was five seven, weighed a mere 143 pounds, and had been diagnosed with emphysema.

"You, my dear man," the doctor said, "are hardly fit for breathing, let alone diving."

Hatzis was unfazed. He went down twice and failed both times, but he remained determined. On his third attempt, he found the anchor and passed a rope through its eye, then surfaced to wild cheers.

Less than a week after Vincenzo returned to Italy, I received a letter from him. He sounded very excited. He said he had been making inquiries in Italy, and he felt that I could make a big splash there as a free diver. He gave me all the particulars—the names of the Italian divers, the dates of the next big competition, even the fancy name for an upcoming event: the Blue Olympics—and I immediately went off to see the local government agency in charge of tourism. There wasn't much left of the agency, since Cuba had long since shuttered its popular casinos, but I did my best to talk them into letting me go to Italy to represent El Comandante in the Blue Olympics. "It would be good for the country," I insisted. "I'll make you proud."

They weren't interested. If it had been a *real* Olympic event, maybe, but this Blue Olympics stuff was meaningless. Free diving was a marginal sport. It would be of no use to the Cuban propaganda machine.

I went home to my failing life and my failing marriage. Luisa and I tended to take our frustrations out on each other, and it got to a point where we couldn't be in the same room without arguing. When we finally split up, inevitably, my life didn't improve. I didn't miss her or the arguments, but I found myself becoming increasingly isolated and depressed. There were days when I couldn't get out of bed. I would lie there, staring at the ceiling, feeling trapped and lost. I wondered if I should have stayed in that damn swimming pool, doing laps for El Comandante. But it was too late for that now. It was too late for so much, it seemed.

Eventually I'd pull myself together and go down to the water, which always brought me back from the abyss. Even the sight of the ocean was enough to give me hope.

Audrey diving down underneath
our boat, *Olokun*.

I began to work again, spearing fish and selling it, illegally, to the shopkeepers. If I came across any black coral, I'd take some of that, too, and sell it to the local jewelers.

Every two or three months, a package would arrive from Vincenzo, in Italy. Despite my inability to get out of Cuba, he stayed in touch. He would send me the latest diving magazines, and I would look at the pictures and read the statistics. In my heart, I knew I could do better and go deeper than any of the Italian divers. But how was I ever going to get out of this prison island?

I knew there was a darker side to the sport of free diving, of course. In the magazines Vincenzo sent, I read about various deaths, men killed by overconfidence, men who bit off more meters than they could chew. And even at home, off the waters of Cuba, there were often deaths and injuries among the divers. I'd been friendly with two divers who were destroyed by the sport. One ended up in a wheelchair, felled by the bends. The other had blacked out only a few feet from the surface, and he'd been pulled to safety by friends, but the accident had paralyzed the entire left half of his face and body.

The way I saw it, however, there were risks everywhere. Life itself was a risk. You could die crossing the damn street, especially in downtown Havana. I wanted to be a free diver. I was good at it—it was probably the *only* thing I was good at—and I wanted a chance to prove myself.

One day, in 1987, I heard that the government was going to open a hotel on Cayo Largo, a spit of sand between Cuba and the Cayman Islands. It was the first step in an effort to revitalize the country's lagging tourism industry, and it was a big deal. They had invited forty foreign journalists, and they were putting on a big show: musicians, fire-eaters, dancers, singers. The event also included an underwater photography competition, and some of the best people in the business were going to compete. I desperately wanted to be part of this international event.

I went to see my old friends at the tourism office and practically fell to my knees. Free diving was a *real* sport, I explained. The European journalists understood this. Why not let me try to set a world record?

The previous year, an Italian free diver, Estefano Macula, had reached a depth of sixty-three meters, but I knew I could go deeper.

After much deliberation, they actually agreed to give me a chance. After all, what did they have to lose? If nothing else, the visitors might find me mildly entertaining.

I was beside myself with excitement, and I began to plan my dive.

There are basically three approaches to the sport. The first is Constant Weight, in which the diver must use his own body, with no artificial weight, to swim to the deepest possible spot, then fight his way back to the surface under his own steam. The second, a name I came up with in 1992, is Variable Weight, where the diver uses a sled to get to the bottom, but must return on his own power, either by swimming or by pulling himself up along the line. And the third is No Limits, where the diver uses a weighted sled to travel to his target, then rockets back to the surface with the help of a balloon.

I was a newcomer to the sport, and—beyond what I'd read in the diving magazines—I didn't know much about either No Limits or Variable Weight. And I certainly didn't have the necessary equipment. So I relied solely on my own body, without any artificial weights.

On the appointed day, with a great deal of fanfare, and in front of a very impressive crowd, I filled my lungs to bursting and plunged into the water. Less than two minutes later, I surfaced, having reached a depth of sixty-seven meters—a new world record. The foreign journalists went wild—they knew what this meant—but the Cuban reporters were a little confused. They didn't fully understand the sport, or the significance of my accomplishment.

Still, a few nights later, at a hotel in Havana, the government had a small party for me. They gave me a diving watch and a nice pat on the back, then sent me on my way, back to the streets.

Within a few days, however, my photograph and accounts of the record-setting dive were finding their way into European magazines. Suddenly, I was Pipín Ferreras, the record-setting free diver. It didn't matter that people in Cuba didn't know much about the sport; in Europe they knew who I was and understood the magnitude of my achievement. I was part dolphin, the foreigners said. I was a human submarine.

That fateful dive, launched largely as cheap entertainment, actually changed the course of my entire life. Suddenly I was a national hero, albeit on a very small scale. *A hero of the revolution.* The government couldn't afford to have a young man of my stature making his living off the waters of the Malecón, so they gave me a paying job at the dive shop at El Pelicano, the hotel on Cayo Largo where I'd performed. I started giving diving lessons to wealthy tourists. Some of them had actually heard of me, amazingly enough, and the others heard about me soon enough: I carried a collection of magazine and newspaper clippings in my back pocket, and I wasn't shy about showing them around.

Before long, I was back in the good graces of my old military friends. I was invited aboard their yachts and into their homes. I was fun to have around. And, if nothing else, when you went spearfishing with Pipín, you never went home empty-handed.

It was here, at El Pelicano, some time later, that I met Simona, a beautiful Italian woman who ran a travel agency in the hotel lobby. She was twenty-nine, and a bit of an idealist. She had come to Cuba because she believed in communism, and in the country's future. She also believed in me, as it turned out, and in motherhood, and before I knew it—at age twenty-six—I was giving marriage another chance.

One balmy afternoon we went off to see a justice of the peace, just the two of us, and returned to her apartment as man and wife. It had happened so fast that for a time I didn't believe it myself, but at the end of the day I felt pretty good about my life. I had a wife, a decent job, and I was about to try for another record . . .

When I actually broke the record a few months later, with a sixty-nine-meter dive, and in front of a substantial crowd, the government began to take me more seriously. Maybe there was something to this crazy sport, after all. Maybe it was worth sending the kid abroad.

I was filled with wild optimism.

Cuba was a beautiful country, and life was a beautiful thing.

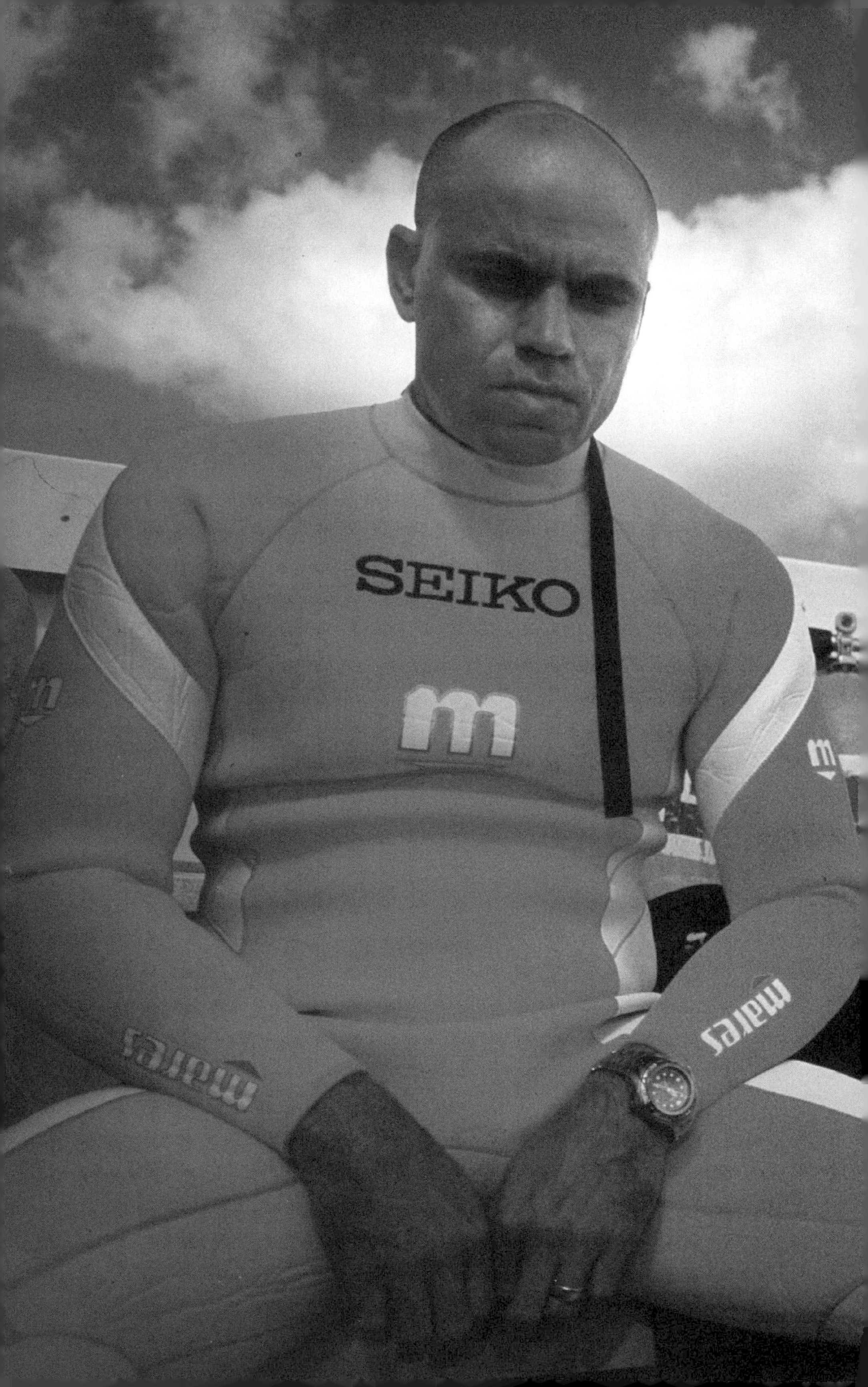
SEIKO
mares
mares

↓

Chapter_ FOUR:

THE WIDE WIDE WORLD OF SPORT

In Cozumel, where I set the No Limits record.

I left Cuba for the first time in 1989, at the age of twenty-nine, to go to Sicily for a free-diving competition. I was accompanied by an entourage of Cuban military officers, including several expert divers, who were there, in part, to make sure I returned to my homeland when the championship was over.

I had every intention of returning. Cuba was being very, very good to me. My goal on this trip was to break the world record in the No Limits category, which had been set earlier that year by a woman, Italy's Angela Bandini. She had ridden a sled down to an astonishing 107 meters.

As I explained earlier, No Limits means that there are no restrictions on the amount of weight a diver carries on his or her descent. Constant Weight, on the other hand, restricts the diver to using the same amount of weight on the way up and down, so there's a very clear limit to how much ground he or she can cover in such a short span of time.

I had started out as a Constant Weight diver, largely because I didn't have access to the technology I needed. But I had become increasingly interested in No Limits. The reason for this is that, for me, and for others like me, it all boils down to one simple, overriding question: *How deep can a man dive on a single breath of air?* And the answer comes down, in part, to a question of speed. The faster you can reach your target, the sooner you can turn around and come back for air.

From a technical standpoint, from the point of view of getting you to the bottom, and getting you there *fast,* there were many years of trial and error. Divers tried strapping more and more weight to their bodies. They built steel contraptions that pulled them head first through the water, threatening to rip their arms out of their sockets. They kept inventing any number of Rube Goldberg–like devices, all of which invariably failed to do the job. But then the aluminum sled came along and changed everything. It was like an aquatic ski lift, though ski *drop* would be more accurate. The diver, wearing only a wet suit, fins, and a nose clip, shot toward the bottom, head first. Once there, he would disconnect the weights, reach for the tank of compressed air on the pole above his head, inflate a balloonlike lift bag with the twist of a valve, and rocket back to the surface.

Before long, No Limits had really taken off. It was a little crazy, admittedly, but once you'd taken the plunge you didn't even think of going back to Constant Weight. I was hooked, frankly. My biggest problem with the sport, back in those early days, was purely technical. The sled hadn't been perfected yet, and—like my counterparts overseas—I was busy designing and building models of my own. I made several out of welded bed frames, but the salt water destroyed them in very short order. I kept trying, though. I knew this was the sport for me, and I eventually helped design a version of the sled that is in use to this day—the one that puts the diver in an upright, sitting position, with his or her legs hooked around the sled's crossbar.

As the sport grew in popularity, so too did the criticism. People said No Limits was a circus act. Stunt work, not athletics. They said it was the least "pure" form of free diving.

At one point, the World Confederation of Underwater Sport actually stopped sanctioning No Limits records, dismissing the practice as too dangerous. But that was part of it, wasn't it? Pushing the envelope. Going to the edge. Finding out what you were capable of. Testing the inner you.

There was also a less philosophical reason for taking the plunge, at least in my case: I wanted to go *where no man had gone before.*

I was a long way from reaching my destination, of course. I was a relative newcomer to the No Limits business, but I knew I'd found my calling. So as soon as I got to Sicily, I went off to the town of Siracusa to look for Enzo Maiorca, the No Limits master, the man they called the Lion.

Audrey, arms stretched taut, rocketing back to the surface.

I found him training on a huge navy ship, two hundred yards off-shore, and I plunged into the chilly Mediterranean—much to the chagrin of my safety divers—and swam out to meet him.

When I reached Maiorca's boat, I was helped aboard by a man who identified himself as Salvatore Trapani, a representative of Mares, the hugely successful diving-equipment company. And when Maiorca surfaced, a trim, leather-skinned man in his late fifties, Trapani introduced us. "Enzo, this is Pipín Ferreras, the Cuban kid. Pipín, Enzo."

That evening, I was breaking bread with Maiorca. I couldn't believe it. One of my heroes, a man I'd glimpsed in my long-ago youth, a man I'd read about in magazines and newspapers, the god of free diving, and there he was, directly across the table. He served me a heaping dish of *linguini mare,* pasta topped with seafood. This wasn't possible. Maiorca was behaving like a regular person; he seemed almost *human.*

"I hear you are pretty good, eh?" he said in broken Spanish.

"I'm working on it," I said. What else could I say? I was actually *humbled* in his presence. The man had been setting records for almost three decades. The fact that he was fifty-eight and semiretired didn't make him less of a giant.

"So when will we see what you are made of?" he barked.

On November 2, 1989, I dove into the chilly waters off the cape of Milazzo. The Mediterranean is a good deal colder than the Caribbean, and the water is much saltier, which makes you more buoyant. This is not good. Buoyancy is the enemy. It slows you down. And because the water's heavier, the pressure on your ears and body is that much greater. I tried not to think about any of this on my way down, and I guess I succeeded. When it was all over, I had set the No Limits world record of 112 meters.

That's what I was made of. The Cuban had arrived.

If you want to learn about bullfighting, go to Spain. If free diving is your sport, the place for you is Italy.

After that first trip, Italy became my home away from home. With Cuba's blessing, Simona and I took a small apartment in Bologna, where she was a university student. After all, I had become El Comandante's unofficial Ambassador of Diving, a walking advertisement for the pristine waters and sugar-smooth beaches of our tropical island paradise, and I had to go abroad to spread the word. I was on fire. Even Mares, the world's largest manufacturer of diving equipment, had given me its blessing, sponsoring me to the tune of $20,000—a bloody fortune.

I learned how to speak Italian. I went to dive shops, seminars, and trade shows across the country, drumming up business for El Comandante. *The beaches in Cuba are unbeatable! The water so clear you can see for miles! The fish are as big as Russian submarines!*

Every few weeks I'd fly back to Cuba, where I still had a job at El Pelicano, and where I continued giving diving classes, many of them to some of the hundreds of Italians I had lured to our island paradise.

I was having the time of my life, to be honest. I was a minor celebrity. People recognized me on the street, asked me to pose for pictures, bought me drinks at the poolside bar. I loved the attention. My parents may have neglected me during those early, formative years, but now I was *somebody*.

Of course, I was an even bigger somebody in Italy, and it was there, in that Mecca of free diving, the home of my chosen sport, that I would have to try to turn myself into an international star. Italy is where it all began, in fact—this crazy notion that men could dive to set records, not just for pleasure. This was where, in 1949, Raimondo Bucher, an expatriate Hungarian, set the first sanctioned mark in the sport. Wearing a mask, fins, and a rudimentary metal snorkel, Bucher descended to thirty meters—and suddenly the race was on; the race to go deeper than any man had ever gone before.

For the next decade, Bucher and two Italians, Enio Falco and Alberto Noveli, kept breaking their own and each other's records, until Brazil's Amerigo Santarelli blew them out of the water in 1960 by descending to an astonishing forty-four meters. That record didn't last, however. Later that same year, a wiry Sicilian by the name of Enzo Maiorca put them all to shame by reaching fifty meters.

Maiorca dominated the sport until the late 1960s, when two new-comers appeared on the scene. One was Jacques Mayol, the famous Frenchman; the other was a U.S. Navy diver named Robert Croft. Croft had freakishly large lungs—with a reported capacity of nine liters—and was said to be the inspiration for the TV series *Aquaman.* In 1967, he gave the sport a boost in the United States with a sixty-six-meter dive off the coast of Fort Lauderdale, which he accomplished in a record two minutes, six seconds.

But it was the Mayol-Maiorca rivalry that gave the sport its person-ality. They were the Ali and Frazier of free diving. For twenty years, the record kept passing between them, each man determined to prove he was the best, neither of them willing to relinquish the title.

Maiorca was the innovator, constantly tinkering with sled design, experimenting with wet suits, even stuffing his mask with wax to reduce "face squeeze." Mayol was the intellectual. Mind over body. He intro-duced yoga and meditation techniques. He spoke of man's primal con-nection to sea mammals and wrote the book *Homo Delphinus,* which years later so enchanted Audrey.

Mayol and Maiorca were also the inspiration for *Le Grand Bleu,* Luc Besson's movie, a film that did for free diving what *Endless Summer* did for surfing. It gave the fringe sport a mainstream following.

Besson's depiction of the Mayol-Maiorca rivalry was half fiction and half bad acting, but the cinematography was hypnotic. It was a popular hit in France and remains a cult favorite around the world.

And understandably so. To me, Mayol and Maiorca were the fathers of free diving. I had already met Maiorca, over a steaming plate of home-made *linguini mare,* and now it was time to meet Mayol.

From everything I'd heard, Mayol was a much more elusive charac-ter. He had retired in 1983, at the age of fifty-six, after setting his final record of 105 meters. At that point, he had lost interest in what he con-sidered his "overhyped" rivalry with Maiorca, and had turned his atten-tion almost exclusively to hard science. Not that it had ever been far from his mind. When he broke the hundred meter mark in 1976, the free-diving equivalent of a four-minute mile, doctors and scientists had predicted that the pressure would crush his thoracic cavity like an empty soda can.

"How did you know you would survive the pressure?" I asked him.

I was finally in front of the great man, at his villa in Elba, the tiny, fish-shaped island off the west coast of Italy, where Napoleon had been exiled in 1814, and this was the first thing I asked him.

"From the dolphins," he said. "I learned everything from the dolphins."

Born in Shanghai to French parents, Mayol developed an early affinity for the sea during the long steamship voyages to and from France. When he left home, it wasn't to settle down, but to explore the world. He was a lumberjack, a miner, a radio commentator, a pianist, and—during World War II—an interpreter for the French Air Force. But he never strayed far from the sea.

In the early 1960s, his travels brought him to Florida, where he took a job as a diver and dolphin trainer at the Miami Seaquarium. One afternoon, a dolphin named Clown looked straight into Mayol's eyes "with what I can only describe as an expression of great tenderness. It was as though she recognized me," he went on, "as though she wanted to tell me something."

Clown, who subsequently gave birth to the more famous Flipper, became Mayol's guide, and they began spending countless hours together. They swam and played and fooled around and Mayol tried to hold his breath for ever-longer periods.

"I was riveted by her sheer joy of living," he said. "I wondered if we humans were capable of that type of unadulterated happiness."

Mayol was a surprisingly slight man. He was gray and weathered, with a tidy stripe of a mustache that gave him a dapper, impish appearance, and he had a faraway look in his eyes. He told me he was happiest in the water, which I, of course, could immediately relate to. "I've always said I feel more at home in the water than I do on dry land," I told him.

Audrey, Pascal, and me in Spain.

"But of course," he replied. "Life began in the ocean 3.7 billion years ago. Our memories of our aquatic origins are imbedded in our genes. In some people, people like us, those memories are simply much more pronounced."

It was a relief to be able to talk to Jacques Mayol about these things. Too often, people dismissed me as a crackpot, or worse. But Mayol was a scientist. It was wonderful to know that a man of science understood and embraced the more esoteric aspects of our chosen sport.

In the early days, however, when he was still a young man, before he began to explore these spiritual dimensions, it had been pure science for Mayol. At Seaquarium, for example, during autopsies on dolphins, he discovered that there was nothing in their anatomy to prevent their chests from collapsing under extreme pressure. He further noted that their lungs were eerily similar to our own. "I thought, *Whatever protects them at great depths must surely protect us, too,*" he said.

In later years, he became something of an underwater guinea pig. Scientists studied his body during dives. He wore a cardiac catheter and his heart rate slowed from 60 beats per minute to 27. When he broke the magical hundred-meter mark, scientists were finally able to observe the phenomenon we've come to know as *blood shift.* Mayol's body responded to water pressure just like a dolphin's body. Every blood vessel in his body constricted, pushing the blood toward his chest cavity and filling his lungs, which had shrunk to a quarter of their normal size. Because liquid is not compressible, the blood kept his rib cage from being crushed.

Oddly enough, the entire blood shift process actually kicks into gear the minute a person steps into the water. Scientists coined a term for it: the *mammalian dive reflex.* As soon as one enters the water, the nerve receptors go to work to conserve oxygen. Blood is shunted to vital organs, the limbs stop burning fuel, the heart gears down, pacing itself, and the spleen begins spitting out oxygen-rich red blood cells.

"It's all about oxygen," Mayol explained. "The body responds immediately because the body is a lot smarter than we imagine."

Mayol went to China to study Pranayama yoga. If it was all about oxygen, then it was all about breathing, and he thought he could become a better diver if he learned how to breathe properly. The yogis taught him how to control his breathing, and how to find that special place deep inside himself that was free of stress and static. "They taught me that the key to holding my breath was to forget that I was holding it," he explained. "And that is the place where there truly are 'No Limits.' "

Shortly after I returned to Cuba, where I was still working at El Pelicano, an Italian free diver arrived one afternoon, looking for me. His name was Umberto Pelizzari. He was tall, blond, lanky, and three years my junior. He was from the small inland town of Busto Arsizio, where he had been so terrified of water as a child that he cried in the bathtub. His mother put him in swimming class to help him overcome his fear.

Now, years later, he was beginning to make something of a name for himself in free diving. He thought he would improve if we trained together, if we pushed each other to the limit. And he already had one world record to his name, not in free diving but in static apnea: he had lain submerged in a swimming pool and held his breath for a full five minutes.

In those early days, Pelizzari and I had a lot in common. I showed him the sights in Cuba and he did the same for me in Italy. But we were both ambitious, and—with Mayol and Maiorca no longer in the picture—there was a huge void in the sport.

"Someday, Pipín," Pelizzari said. "It will be you and me."

"Maybe," I said. "People always love a good rivalry, whether it's politics or sport."

We could not foresee how our friendship would be destroyed by our competitiveness, by a rivalry that would drive both of us closer and closer to the center of the earth.

In 1990, at the age of twenty-eight, Simona gave birth to Francisca, an adorable little girl. She had her mother's rotini curls and my round face, which made for a very nice combination (if I may say so myself).

The one thing that colored the joys of fatherhood was the sad fact that my relationship with Simona had begun to suffer. I no longer understood love. I had been in love twice, or at least I *thought* I'd been in love, and both times I'd fallen out of love in very short order. We were civil with each other, and we took our responsibilities as parents very seriously, but the romance was gone. I continued to work at the hotel, tending to a steady stream of tourists, and Simona did her work for the travel agency and tried to help turn my interest in free diving into a career. Instead of husband and wife, we had become business partners. She was oddly capitalistic for a woman who believed so strongly in Cuba, but that suited me just fine.

Shortly after Francisca was born, I heard from Sector, the Swiss watchmaker, who wondered if I'd be interested in endorsing a line of sport watches. As they saw it, I had changed the face of the sport. For one thing, I was the one who had came up with the idea of riding the sled in an upright, sitting position, instead of head first. For another, they seemed to like my bald head and brash personality, though not necessarily in that order. They wanted to launch a *No Limits* line of sport watches, and they wanted to pay me $50,000 for the honor. I was in heaven, and so was Simona. She saw this as the beginning of something really big.

"You've got to get on TV," she said. "You're nobody until you get on TV."

It was Simona who organized my next dive, in July 1991, off the coast of Siracusa, Italy, and it was Simona who made sure it was broadcast live, on European television. It was quite a production, too. Six cameramen were placed in the water, staggered at deeper and deeper intervals along the line, and they captured every phase of the descent. It was the first underwater production of its kind, and it turned out to be a huge success. The fact that I reached a new record of 115 meters certainly helped.

It was a strange existence. I was traveling between two worlds and two very different societies. Italy was a land of plenty; Cuba, my home, was defined by its terrible poverty.

On the beach in the Dominican Republic, en route to the boat and loaded down with dive cables.

In a way, I began to feel like a stranger in my own country. I would return from Italy with the sorts of luxuries most Cubans couldn't even dream of. Nice clothes, electronic equipment, toys for my baby. My wallet was full of dollars. I had a real bank account in Italy, three credit cards, and a Cuban passport. And I had an Italian wife, at least nominally, so I figured I'd apply for an Italian passport, too. You never knew when it might come in handy.

Try as we might, Simona and I remained estranged, but she was a good partner, and a smart negotiator, and business was good. One day I got this crazy notion that I could get the government to let me open up my own dive shop, right there in Havana, at the Hotel Commodore. And I knew a way around the strict laws that forbade Cubans from owning private property: we would put the whole operation in Simona's name. She was a foreigner, so those particular laws didn't apply to her.

In Cuba, a decision of that magnitude could only be made by one man, and I had the connections. I went to my military friends and asked them to try to set up a meeting with El Comandante. It wasn't as outrageous as it sounded. Castro knew all about me. He read the papers. And in his youth he had been an avid spearfisherman himself.

One afternoon, I got a phone call telling me to wait outside my house at 2 A.M. In the dead of night, a black Mercedes came to pick me up and took me to one of Castro's many houses. I had seen him before—at a recent event promoting tourism, and at various (mandatory) political functions over the years—but this was the first time we were in a room together, face-to-face.

He looked fit and strong, almost bearlike, and he was warm and friendly. The first thing he did was show me the architectural plans for two new resorts that were being financed by a business consortium in Madrid. Then we sat down and talked a little about free diving, about Italy, and about the latest spearfishing guns on the market—a far cry from the old-fashioned, rubber-band-style *escopetas de liga* he remembered from his youth.

Finally, it was time to make my pitch. I told him about opening a dive shop, and about putting it under the name of my Italian wife, and I suggested sharing the profits equally with the state.

"Last year alone, I lured more than two thousand Italian divers to Cuba," I said. "This is paradise to them. Let's make it work for us."

Castro was a businessman, and he was nobody's fool. Plus the country was in serious trouble. When the Soviet Union disintegrated, Cuba lost the subsidies that had kept it going, if only barely, for thirty years (40 billion dollars, according to some estimates). The country's illusions about socialism as a viable economic system had proven to be just that: illusions. Cuba was in a serious depression, though El Comandante preferred to call it a "special period of sacrifice."

As a result, our fearless leader had begun to flirt with capitalism. One of his first ventures involved Pablo Milanes, a respected local musician. Milanes opened a recording studio in Havana, but he did so under the name of his manager, a Uruguayan, thereby skirting the private-ownership laws. They were making money and sharing the proceeds with the government. It was working. Everyone was happy. I was hoping Castro would do the same for me.

At the end of the evening, Castro stood and put his arm around my shoulders. *"Okay, Pipín, vamos a ver lo que podemos hacer,"* he said. "Let's see what we can do. But it's our own, secret experiment, so take it slow."

He walked me to the door and said he'd be in touch.

I couldn't believe it. I sat in the back of the Mercedes for the drive home in a complete daze. I felt like a real entrepreneur!

I woke Simona when I got home. She couldn't believe it, either. This was a dream come true. We were actually being given the freedom to make something of our lives, right there at home, in Cuba.

But nothing happened. Some high-ranking military men decided it was a bad idea, and they worked behind the scenes to make sure it never got beyond the planning stages. They felt I had somehow breached protocol by going directly to Fidel. They didn't like the notion of some punk civilian running around town like a capitalist.

I was angry and frustrated, and for the first time I thought seriously about leaving Cuba. But I had enough things on my plate to keep me busy, so I funneled my anger into my work. I went back to Italy later that year to host a twelve-part TV series on water sports, *Emotions in Blue*. I received $50,000 in sponsorship money from Mercatoni, a big grocery-store chain, and signed up with Sector for another year. The original campaign had been wildly successful, so they doubled the stipend.

"I guess I didn't turn out to be such a bum after all," I told my mother on a rare visit to her house.

"No, Pipín," she said. "I knew you'd make something of your life, and I'm very proud of you. I always knew it was just a matter of time."

Indeed, by now I was what Cubans called an *intocable:* an untouchable. I had money, and I was buying cars and houses, but it was all a bizarre shell game. I didn't really *own* the houses, not on paper, anyway. On paper, everything belonged to foreign companies that didn't even exist, though they certainly appeared to. *On paper.*

Before long, I had five houses, a nice chunk of seaside property, and six cars in Cuba. I should have been happy, but I couldn't escape the misery that surrounded me. The starving children, the beggars, the hungry dogs burrowing through the piles of garbage in the downtown alleys. The entire island was overwhelmed by a sort of collective depression. Once again, I began to think about leaving.

In 1991, my marriage to Simona ended. She took Francisca and moved to Florence. I missed my daughter, if not my wife, and I threw myself into a new relationship with Yamile, a gorgeous woman I'd met through a fellow diver.

Yamile was wild, and quite the rebel, and right from the start it was a very tempestuous relationship. But I couldn't help myself. She was so *different;* so unlike Simona. She liked drinking and dancing and partying, and seldom went to bed before dawn. She also happened to be the first woman I'd ever met who had a diamond stud in her nose, something unheard of in Cuba.

Sometimes I couldn't keep up with her, and we fought. It was like trying to tame a wild animal. When I introduced her to my mother, she didn't approve, and less than a week later, after doing a little investigating, she called to tell me to be careful: the government didn't like the crowd that Yamile ran with, she said. They were keeping an eye on my little girlfriend.

In 1993, with the government's blessing, and at my own expense, I went to the United States for the first time to attend a diving trade show in Orlando. I had recently gotten into underwater photography, and had even managed to sell some beautiful shots to *National Geographic,* and one of the reasons for the trip was to have a look at the latest equipment. The government relented; they knew they could trust their Ambassador of Diving.

As a young boy, and as a Cuban, I had always been taught that America was the enemy, and that the American people were uncouth savages. Part of me knew that this was largely propaganda, but the communist indoctrination had worked on me at some subconscious level, so I went with trepidation.

But it was love at first sight. I loved the clean streets. I loved the manicured parks. I loved the huge, gleaming cars and the smiling, happy people. I loved the stores, stocked with everything imaginable and with some things that were *beyond* my imagination. I loved the pretty women. I even loved my first Big Mac.

Alas, I was only there for two days. Right after the trade show, I flew back to Cuba to prepare for a much-publicized dive with my Italian "archenemy," Umberto Pelizzari. Two months later, we were standing in front of the Mediterranean, shaking hands for the cameras, but it turned out not to be much of a competition. Pelizzari opted for Constant Weight, and I went for No Limits. He plunged into the frigid waters and reached a depth of 73 meters, a record for that branch of the sport. The Italians went wild. Then I went down on a sled and hit 120 meters, another record. The Italians cheered, if slightly less boisterously. On the whole, however, the media was happy. They saw this as the beginning of a beautiful rivalry, and they were going to milk it for all it was worth. Pelizzari and I understood this only too well. We wanted to milk it, too. After all, without the media, we were nothing.

I returned to Cuba with a new record and a new toy: a silver, 1600 cc Suzuki motorcycle. I had a little trouble at customs, but I called an old friend in the military and soon found myself out in the streets, roaring from one end of the island to the next.

Yamile loved our new toy. "Faster!" she would say, clinging on for dear life. "Faster!"

I racked up fifteen speeding tickets in the space of two weeks, and I could never bite my tongue with those damn cops. "Do you know who I am? I am Pipín Ferreras, *brodel,* world champion free diver! I have friends in high places. Even *Fidel* is a close personal friend!"

All right. I admit it. Success went to my head. And I paid the price.

Before long, I was persona non grata. I'm not sure what happened exactly, but I think some of my old cronies in the military began to see me as a spoiled kid who lived better than they did. Others still resented the fact that I had gone directly to El Comandante with my plans for the Hotel Commodore, although it was obvious by now that that idea was going nowhere.

Suddenly I could no longer get any of my contacts on the phone, and it worried me. I felt I was being watched. I remembered what my mother had said about Yamile. I wondered whether that was part of it. At any moment now, the government could turn on me. I would be a nonperson, or worse: *an enemy of the revolution.*

I began to think about defecting to the United States, and that worried me, too. In Cuba, a man could be arrested for just *thinking* about defecting. I was in a bad place. The one thing I loved above all else was free diving, and the government was allowing me to indulge my passion, but I was doing it on their terms—and not under the best of circumstnaces. I needed better equipment, and the money to buy it. I had spent nearly everything I'd earned. I needed a generous sponsor. And I needed all of this to happen fast. I was thirty-one years old. How many good years did I have left?

Audrey during a deep part of a practice dive, only days before her fatal accident.

I have never been a political person, but the politics were killing me. I was living a lie. I hated the hypocrisy. I felt like climbing to the highest rooftops and shouting out the truth for all to hear. I wanted to tell my fellow Cubans that it was over, that Castro's revolution had failed. But of course you couldn't do that in Cuba. You couldn't even do it *privately.* You never knew if your neighbor or the guy at the corner store was working for the Committee for the Defense of the Revolution. I could trust no one. And I could share my thoughts with no one. Cuba was coming apart at the seams. Even the true believers were becoming disenchanted. Vladimiro Roca, a former leader of the Communist Party, had been jailed simply for advocating change. There was plenty of irony in that: Lenin's namesake rotting behind bars, a political prisoner. And he was just one of hundreds.

And what about the tens of thousands who risked their lives on flimsy, homemade rafts, trying to escape to a better life in America? Since the revolution, an estimated one million people—fully a tenth of the population—had abandoned Cuba.

I found it bizarre—the way people held on to their failed dreams. The government liked to boast that there was one doctor for every 166 Cubans, and maybe that was true. But what they didn't tell you is that there wasn't enough medicine or modern equipment to let them do their jobs. And Fidel liked to say that the Cuban people were among the most educated, literate people in the world, and maybe there was some truth to that, too. But what good is an education when it's restricted to propaganda about Marxism and socialism, and to outright lies about the evils of capitalism?

It dawned on me that the people who still believed in the revolution were living in denial. They had more and lived better than the rest of the population, making it easier to deny that anything was wrong. Not for me. And I had plenty—for a Cuban. Too much, in fact. Way more than my fair share. But I didn't have my freedom. My freedom was just out of grasp, across the Straits of Florida.

Italy was another option, to be sure, especially since I had an Italian passport, but it seemed so far away. And in Miami, hell—the air itself *felt* Cuban. I'd be exiled but not alone. I could speak Spanish in Miami. I could eat rice and beans. I could get a good cup of Cuban coffee at every other corner. And Yamile even had family in Miami.

"What's keeping us here?" I asked Yamile one night, as we lay in bed, drifting off to sleep.

"What are you talking about?" she asked.

"You ever think about Miami?" I asked.

"All the time," she said. "I have an uncle in Miami, and I hear he's doing great."

In November 1993, I was scheduled to go to Freeport, in the Bahamas, to represent the Cuban government in an international underwater photo competition. I had my Italian passport, so I knew I wouldn't have much trouble defecting, but I wasn't going to leave Yamile behind. With the help of one of my last remaining friends in the Cuban military, as well as the British consul, whom I'd taken spearfishing a few times, I secured a tourist visa for Yamile and took her to Freeport with me. Shortly after we arrived, her uncle showed up on a chartered plane and snuck her into Miami. I followed the next day, on a commercial flight, and breezed right through customs with my Italian passport.

Yamile and her uncle were waiting for me at the airport, but before we left I found a pay phone and called my mother in Cuba. She'd already heard about my defection, and she was crying. "I'm sorry," I told her. "This was the right thing for me to do. I hope you understand."

"I don't know if I'll ever understand," she replied. "Maybe it's my fault."

"Mom, don't say that. This has nothing to do with you."

"You're wrong," she insisted. "Maybe if I hadn't been so caught up in the revolution, maybe if I'd been home more, maybe if I'd been more of a mother, this never would have happened. You had to run off and take comfort in the sea."

"Then you did a good thing," I said. "I love the sea."

Yamile and I followed her uncle out of the terminal and into the parking lot, then got into his car for the drive to Miami. I was excited, but I was also nervous, and I became more nervous when we reached her uncle's house. It was a rundown motor home, not exactly what I'd been expecting. It had begun to rain by this time, and the motor home leaked. I remember looking for a dry corner in which to set my bag, and asking myself, "What the hell have I done?"

The next day, after a nice cup of Cuban coffee, I went to the bank and discovered that Simona had canceled my credit cards and closed all of my accounts in Italy. She was mad, and I could understand why. I wouldn't leave Cuba to join her in Italy, but I had left the country for Yamile.

I went back to the motor home and told Yamile the bad news. "All I've got to my name is two pairs of jeans, four shirts, two cameras, some slightly used snorkeling gear, and about five hundred dollars."

"What are we going to do?" she asked.

The following day, we drove down to the Keys, which hang off the tip of Florida like the tail on a kite. It is a haven for divers, who are attracted to the area by two beautiful state parks—John Pennekamp and Biscayne National—and by the only living coral reef in the continental United States. The highway was lined with dive shops and I stopped to talk to a few of the owners and employees.

"I'm a free diver," I told them.

They stared at me blankly, as if I'd said I was a Martian. I explained who I was and exactly what I did.

"Why would you want to do *that*?" one man asked me.

No one was even remotely interested in my free diving, but if I knew how to dive with tanks and pump gas and clean boats, they said, they had a job for me. I signed on. They paid cash.

"We'll never go hungry," I told Yamile. "We'll be fine."

But Yamile wasn't happy. In Cuba, I'd been a real somebody. Here, in America, I was a complete nobody. Or worse.

"I'm miserable," she said.

"I hear you," I said. "I'm doing the best I can."

We scraped a few dollars together and found a shabby, one-bedroom apartment in Kendall. I was thirty-three years old and starting from scratch as an immigrant, and things weren't moving very quickly, but I had more faith—and more patience—than she did. We argued and reconciled and argued some more.

In June 1994, I went back to Italy for the Blue Olympics, but this time I wasn't representing Cuba or anyone else. I was representing me, Pipín Ferreras—a boat jockey from Miami, a working stiff. Umberto Pelizzari was there, and the press was once again rooting for the hometown boy. We played along, and let them make a big fuss about the coming battle, but I took home the crown this time, breaking my own No Limits record by a single meter. I had reached a depth of 126 meters, enough to win that badly needed first prize check of $30,000.

I went back to Miami and celebrated with Yamile. Within a month, I bought a dive franchise in Key Largo with a fellow Cuban, an investor, and we called it Pipín Divers. It was located at Mile Marker 100, on the ocean side of U.S. 1. We had a dive boat and a Cuban café, and I made a deal to sell diving gear for Mares, the manufacturer.

As it turned out, I was a lousy capitalist and a worse businessman. The operation was a comedy of errors. The guys I hired were unreliable, the boat never left on time, and when we were out at sea we'd always discover that we'd forgotten something crucial—food, for example; or cold drinks. I was losing money to my better organized competitors, and I didn't have any money to lose.

That's when Carlos Serra showed up. I had met him years earlier, in Venezuela, where I'd gone to give a short course in free diving, and now I found him managing a pristine, well-run dive shop three miles down the road. He was doing well, and he could see I was having trouble.

"Pipín, *hombre,* what is so complicated about this?" he said. "These people are tourists, here to enjoy themselves. Just take them out and show them a good time."

"I don't know how," I said. "I'm a free diver, not a tour operator. I'm not cut out for this shit. I don't have the patience for it."

Just as I was about to chuck the whole thing, somebody in the Florida Department of Tourism decided to fund a No Limits dive right

A photo taken by Audrey.

there in Key Largo. I was the first to sign up, and when the big day came I pushed my previous record by a meter and a half, to 127.5 meters. The event got good media coverage, and I appeared on camera. I gave them a few sound bites in my broken English, and left feeling pretty good. There was hope, after all. Maybe we could make this sport happen right here in the United States. This was the land of opportunity, and opportunity had just knocked.

Unfortunately, Yamile still wasn't happy. As far as she was concerned, we'd been better off in Cuba, where at least I counted for something. Here I was just another loser immigrant, struggling to make it with all the other losers. We fought bitterly, and then we reconciled with equal fervor. Maybe too much fervor: one day she walked in and told me that she was pregnant. She didn't look happy about that, either.

"This is a good thing, Yamile," I told her. "It means we have a future. We're going to make it, baby."

"Yeah," she said, pouting. "Sure."

"Come on, woman. *Un poco confianza.*" A little confidence.

Shortly thereafter, as if to confirm my optimism, I ran into Jorge Solino, another Cuban from my distant past. Solino was an underwater photographer, a big bald guy, maybe six feet two, and he'd been in Cayo Largo for my very first record seven years earlier. More recently he'd been in Washington, D.C., editing a *National Geographic* film on Cuba's shipwrecks, and had decided to defect. He had moved to Miami and had driven to the Keys to work on a film for the Baltimore Aquarium, and one day a local dive shop owner asked him about his accent.

"I'm from Cuba," Solino said.

"There's another Cuban in a dive shop not far from here," the man told him. "He's insane. All he talks about is free diving. He claims he's the best free diver in the world."

Solino knew right away that the man was talking about me, so he showed up at my dive shop, unannounced.

"What does a guy have to do to get served around here?" he asked, taking a seat at one of the small tables.

I turned around, ready to give this snotty customer a piece of my mind, and I couldn't believe my eyes. "Solino! ¡*Coño!* What the hell are you doing here?"

I took him home to dinner, and introduced him to Yamile, who was already eight months pregnant, and he saw right away that we were having a rough time.

"Pipín, can I be honest with you?"

"What? You're going to tell me I live in a dump. You think I don't know that?"

"I have an idea," he said, ignoring me. "I'm well connected in the film business. How would you like to make underwater videos with me?"

At that point, I would have taken a job bagging groceries. I closed the dive shop and told Solino I was ready to go to work, but Yamile went into labor before we could line anything up, and two months later it was over . . . No, not Solino and I; Yamile and I.

All we had done was fight and scream until the air itself churned with our anger.

"What do you want from me?" I would yell. "I'm doing the best I can!"

"Well, it's not good enough! I'm miserable! I hate it here. We were supposed to be happy."

Sometimes I would look at Yamile and at our infant son and think that she wasn't much more than a child herself. My ex-wife, Simona, had been a real adult. She ran a business and managed a home and my career even, and she knew how to be a mother to Francisca. But Yamile worried me, and because I worried it made me even angrier. I knew it was wrong, but I couldn't help myself. I was angry all the time. About everything and about nothing. I began to suspect that something was seriously wrong with me.

Worse still, as I told Solino, I felt done with this crazy business of love. I didn't believe in it anymore. I'd been in love twice, or so I thought, and both times it had ended badly. I'm sure I was partly to blame on both occasions, but the real culprit, or so it seemed to me, was love itself.

"How can you go from being so besotted with a woman to feeling like you want to punch her in the nose?" I asked Solino.

"That's the way it works, pal," he said. "The higher you go, the harder you fall."

That was as good an answer as any, I guess. Maybe the trick was not to fall at all. "This love stuff only works in the movies," I told him. "I'm not going to let it happen again."

I took Yamile to the bank and gave her all the money we had; every last penny. I helped her find a small apartment in South Beach and took a little place for myself in Miami, a few miles away. I wanted to stay close. I hadn't been much of a father to my daughter, Francisca, and I was going to make damn sure the same thing didn't happen with my son, Luca.

As for Solino, it turned out he was as broke as I was. But his heart was in the right place, so I let him move in with me while he tried to line up some kind of film job. Meanwhile, I took my gear and went down to the beach, and I did what I had done in Cuba to make money: I went spearfishing in the waters off Miami, and I sold my catch to the local merchants. It was a step backward, perhaps, but it paid the rent.

The next thing I knew, Solino and I began talking about turning my regular spear-fishing expeditions into an underwater film. He borrowed the equipment and followed me into the water, and before long we'd put together a crude video: *Ultimate Spear Fishing*. We didn't try to get it into the Sundance Film Festival, but we had managed to make spearfishing look like an exciting, underwater safari, and we sold hundreds of copies of the video through local dive shops. In my favorite scene, I'm about seventy feet down, doing battle with a grouper that was almost as big as me. I had no tanks, of course, and—unlike a Hollywood actor—no double.

We took the tape to New Orleans for the Diving Equipment and Manufacturers Association (DEMA) trade show. It is the dive industry's biggest annual event, and I thought I could use the film to introduce myself, and to push this whole notion of free diving as a sport. It was a tad humiliating. For three days I sat at a table, trying to lure passers-by. "Step right up, ladies and gentlemen. My name is Pipín Ferreras and I would like to talk to you about free diving, the most incredible sport in the history of sport!"

I sounded like a carnival barker. I had nothing to sell but myself and copies of our videotape, which were going for $29.95. I'm not going to tell you how many I sold.

On the last day, my worst day, as I was sitting there feeling sorry for myself, an older man stopped by to chat.

"Pipín Fererras," he said. "I know all about you. One hundred and twenty-seven meters in Key Largo."

"A hundred and twenty-seven *and a half,*" I said, correcting him. "Are you a fan of the sport?"

"I know a little something about it," he said. He was soft-spoken and conservatively dressed. "And I'm intrigued by it."

"Then you're one of the few in this place."

"You should come to Mexico," he said, smiling. "The water is beautiful in Mexico."

"I've been to Mexico," I said. "But they didn't exactly welcome me with open arms. I asked them to sponsor me, and they said they'd be glad to—if I could get the media interested in one of my dives. Well, I called every TV and radio station in the country, and they all told me to go to hell."

At that point, the man burst out laughing. He reached into his pocket and handed me his business card and I turned beet-red. I thought it was a bad joke. The name Emilio Azcarraga was engraved on the card. There was no phone number. No address. Nothing else. But I didn't need anything else. Everyone knew that Azcarraga was the owner of Mexico's Televisa network, as well as one of the richest men in Latin America. In that cutthroat media world, he was known as El Tigre.

I looked beyond him and noticed four beefy men loitering within easy reach. These were his bodyguards. I could see the telltale bulges under their coats. I turned to look at Azcarraga again.

"It—it's a pleasure to meet you, sir," I stammered.

"I think you should try a dive in Cabo San Lucas," he said. "It's a spectacular spot. You're going to love it."

And that's how I ended up in Cabo San Lucas, where I met Audrey Mestre, the woman who changed my life forever.

↓

Chapter_ FIVE:

RAPTURE
OF THE DEEP

Coaching Audrey on the finer points of free diving in Miami.

By the time we got to La Paz to meet Audrey's parents, she knew everything there was to know about me, and then some.

"You still want to go through with this?" I asked.

"Yes," she said. "I'm crazy about you."

Anne Marie and Jean Pierre were waiting for us at Audrey's tiny apartment. She made the awkward introductions and we sat across from each other in the cramped living area. We all knew why we were there.

"I don't understand how this happened," Jean Pierre began. "You two have just met, and now you tell me that you want to go to Miami to live together?"

Neither of us said anything. What was there to say?

"Don't you think this is a bit impulsive?" Jean Pierre went on. "Why throw away your degree for a foolish fling, Audrey? If you move to Miami you may never go back to your career. At least finish your thesis. It's only four short months."

"I can't wait that long," Audrey said. "And it's not a foolish 'fling.' "

He turned to look at me. "Can't you be reasonable? Can't Miami wait?"

"Miami can wait," I said. "But I can't. I'm in love with your daughter, sir. Something magical happened back there in Cabo. It might sound crazy to you, but it's not crazy to me. And I don't want to take any chances; I don't want to risk losing her."

"Audrey?" It was Anne Marie. So far, she had remained silent. But now she wanted to hear from her little girl.

"I want to be with Pipín," Audrey said.

"You're sure about this?"

"No," Audrey said. "How can one be sure about anything? I don't know if it will last a week, a month, or forty years, but I've never felt this way about anyone, and I don't want to risk losing him, either."

This must have been very hard for both of them. Their daughter was barely out of her teens, still very much a child, and her experiences with men had been quite limited. Now she was telling them that she was in love with a big, bald Cuban free diver whose goal in life was to go deeper than any man had ever gone before.

"I know what you're thinking," I said. "And I understand your concern. But I'm going to ask you to trust me. I love your daughter. And this isn't about a week, a month, or forty years. This is forever."

Audrey reached for my hand. Jean Pierre was at a loss for words. Anne Marie was fighting tears.

"I promise I will always take good care of her," I said.

With Audrey by my side, I felt unstoppable.

We drove back to Cabo the following morning, hooked up with the crew, and immediately began to prepare for the big dive. Audrey had agreed to take Massimo's place in the water, and we had to walk her through the technical aspects of her role. This isn't as simple as it sounds. Massimo had been posted at the fifty-meter mark, which is a helluva way down. But we had to test Audrey at twice that depth to make sure she'd be able to handle it.

"Do you understand that very few people ever dive to these depths?" I asked her.

"I get it, Pipín."

"In fact, you may be the first woman to reach that threshold."

"Great," she said, smiling. "I can't wait."

Pepe and I told her that we would take her down to eighty meters, and that we would do so slowly, to give her a chance to get used to it. We dropped weighted ropes into the water so that we could use them to scurry back to the surface if we needed to.

"It's okay to freak out," I told her. "It's really deep. It can be very freaky."

"I'm fine," she said.

When we got in the water, Pepe signaled to me behind her back that we shouldn't go beyond sixty meters. I agreed with him and nodded. We started making our way down, and Audrey set the pace, moving fearlessly and a little too quickly for my liking. I tried to slow her down and kept her close, watching her for the effects of nitrogen narcosis, also known as "rapture of the deep." Divers have been known to do strange and self-destructive things at great depths, such as offering their regulators to fish or dumping their tanks altogether. But Pepe and I had figured out that this can be avoided if they learn to recognize that they are getting narked. To that end, having reached a depth of fifty meters, we gave Audrey a slate on which we had drawn a series of circles. Her job was to draw circles within the circles. She did well and indicated that she wanted to keep going. I looked at Pepe and he shrugged. We kept going.

I stopped her at seventy meters and again handed her the slate. Her drawing was a little wobbly this time, so I indicated that she should switch to the free-flowing regulator by her left shoulder. This second regulator almost forces you to breathe, and helps level things off. She popped it in her mouth and looked across at me, bright eyed and eager, but I motioned that it was time to go back up.

She put her hands together, as if in prayer, and asked to continue. I looked at Pepe again. This woman was unstoppable.

When we reached the ninety-meter mark, Audrey still wanted to keep going. She took the regulator out of her mouth and I freaked, thinking she was losing it. But she leaned close and kissed my cheek and put her regulator back.

What could I do? We went the rest of the way down.

When we resurfaced, I asked her how she felt.

"Great," she said. "I know I got a little disoriented at about seventy meters, but once I got used to it, it was easy. It felt good."

"Do you have any idea how deep we were?" I said, taken aback by her nonchalance.

Audrey in the water in Spain.

"I knew I had nothing to worry about," she said. "You were right there, by my side."

That night, we were supposed to have dinner with Emilio Azcarraga, but I hadn't heard from him. We were in the hotel room, getting dressed, when the phone rang.

"Pipín, it's Emilio," a familiar voice said. "*¿Dónde estás?*"

"I'm right here in my hotel room. Where are you?"

"Can you see the bay from your room?"

I went out to the balcony and looked at the bay. "Yes," I said.

"Can you see me? We're just dropping anchor now."

"No," I said. "All I can see is a cruise ship. Looks like one of those Carnival Cruise Line things."

"No," Azcarraga replied, laughing. "That's my yacht. We'll send someone ashore to get you. He'll be at the wharf."

We went down to the dock and one of the crewmen came to fetch us. As we roared across the water, toward the yacht, I couldn't believe the size of that thing. I found out later that it was the most luxurious private yacht in the world, and that it had been built at a cost of about a hundred and fifty million dollars.

Azcarraga was there to greet us, and introduced us to a friend and associate, Rupert Murdoch, whom I had never heard of. We had dinner and chatted like old friends. I was telling another wild story about my childhood in Cuba when Azcarrraga suddenly interrupted in midsentence. "How would you like to write a book about your life?" he asked.

"A book?"

"Don't worry," he said. "We'll find someone to write it for you. All you have to do is talk."

"Sounds good," I said. "Everyone loves to talk about themselves."

Azcarraga laughed. "There's an old saying," he said. " 'When you find me interesting, you're a genius. When you find yourself interesting, you're a bore.' "

"I'll have to remember that," I said.

He offered me fifty thousand dollars for the book and we shook hands on it, but on the way back to shore that night I wondered if it was real. Then again, I had no reason to doubt Azcarraga. Here I was in Cabo San Lucas, right? Preparing for a new record. And that had been entirely his doing.

The next day, we did one more training dive with Audrey. She was an accomplished diver, though never at this depth, but it was instantly apparent that she would have no trouble handling fifty meters. As I noted earlier, divers are staggered at intervals along the descent route, so that they can lend a hand if anything goes wrong.

The following day, March 10, 1996, I went after the record.

It was a sunny morning. The water of the bay was chilly but smooth. We anchored the dive boat at our practice site, then dropped 130 meters' worth of cable through a pulley on a davit that hung from the side of the boat. The cable was weighted with a hundred-pound anchor, and it dropped like a bullet.

As the divers got ready to go into the water, squeezing into their wet suits and backpacks, I sat in a quiet corner of the boat and concentrated on what lay ahead of me. That is the point at which I go into my predive cocoon, insulating myself from the surrounding activity. I reminded myself that I had hit the mark several days earlier, and that I could do it again. Then I began to relax my body, moving from the top of my head to the tips of my toes. I focused on each set of muscles, willing them to loosen up. I created a mental image of myself: heavy and gravity-bound on land, but quick as a fish underwater. The key is not to fight the ocean, but to let it swallow you whole.

I slid into the water and floated face down, letting the dive reflex take over. My heart rate and breathing slowed. I sat on the crossbar of the sled, which was suspended in the water in the ready position, and began to ventilate, breathing deeply through my mouth. To get used to

A submarine belonging to James Cameron, the film director.

the water pressure, I did three warm-up dives. The first lasted a minute; the second two; the third two and a half. On this last one, I went down to forty meters.

A few more breaths and I hooked my legs round the sled, my head up, out of the water.

"I'm ready," I said.

Audrey and the other safety divers jumped into the water and formed a semicircle around me. I looked at Audrey, at her big brown eyes sparkling behind her mask. She seemed more beautiful to me with each passing day, and even there, in the water, I felt myself bursting with love. It was very strange. I remembered what I had told Solino—that I was never going to let myself fall in love again—and it occurred to me that I hadn't lied to him. I hadn't fallen in love again. I was in love for the very first time in my life.

I wanted to tell Audrey I was absolutely insanely crazy about her, but there was no time. She knew how I felt, anyway, and was probably tired of hearing it. No matter: I would tell her again when I surfaced, and again that night, when we made love.

We began the five-minute countdown, and the deepest diver began his long journey to the bottom. Audrey and the others soon followed him down and I could feel their bubbles rolling up along my legs.

Once they were on their way, the clock was ticking. Divers can only stay at certain depths for an allotted period of time, and if I stalled I would risk putting them in danger. A successful dive requires synchronized teamwork.

I tightened my grip on the sled, clutching it against my chest, breathing slowly. There was a lot of activity around me—the growing number of spectator boats, inching ever closer; photographers and TV commentators, some of them already in mid-broadcast; and my own crew, in and out of the water—but all of that was slowly fading from my consciousness. Before long, I could hear only my own inhalations and exhalations, and within a minute the world around me began to disappear.

The noise. The people. Even the cloud-dappled sky.

I was now entirely focused on the world below me. I asked Olokun, god of the ocean, for the protection he had always granted me in his kingdom.

I picked up the pace of my breathing. By hyperventilating, I was not only revving up my heart rate, but expelling carbon dioxide and saturating my body with oxygen. It would be a long time before I took another breath.

I wrapped the backs of my legs around the crossbar, getting into a kneeling position. I inhaled one more time, first filling my abdomen, then my rib cage, and finally the upper portion of my lungs and larynx. I had crammed 8.2 liters of air into my body, and I was going to need every last molecule of it.

I released the pin that held the sled in place, shut my eyes, and plunged into the deep.

For the first 30 meters, I was moving at about 1.5 meters per second. I kept my nose pinched and blew at regular intervals, as necessary, to equalize the crushing pressure in my ears.

At the 50-meter mark, I figured my heart rate had fallen to 45 beats per minute. At the 80-meter mark, it was closer to 30.

At the 100-meter mark, I whipped past one of my safety divers, who was banging on his tank with a wrench to let me know how far I'd come.

The pressure on my ears became intense, and I had to keep pumping air through my Eustachian tubes to equalize it. If the eardrums rupture, the result is not pretty: extreme dizziness, nausea, and vomiting (not to mention excruciating pain).

At 110 meters, I blew with all my might, but I was out of air by now, so I switched to Plan B. This involved letting go of my nose and allowing the salt water to rush into my sinuses. The water displaced the remaining air and relief was immediate.

The pressure was so intense at this point—13 atmospheres, or 220 pounds per square inch of skin—that I myself was actually physically compressed, and my wet suit, skintight on the surface, was now slightly baggy.

I could feel my lungs shriveling and filling with blood.

For a second, my resolve weakened, but then I heard the last of the safety divers, clanging away in greeting, and I knew I was going to make it. At that point, my heart rate was probably down to about 15 or 20 beats per minute, and at those levels you've got to keep your mind from playing tricks on you. To avoid becoming disoriented, I spelled my name out; I reminded myself that Audrey would be waiting for me on the surface; I assured myself that I was still going *down,* and that in a matter of seconds it would be time to reverse course for the trip back.

My body groaned under the strain. A few more seconds and I was in unexplored territory: I was deeper than any human being on the planet, not only then, but *ever*. At 130 meters, I hit the brakes and the sled came to a jarring halt at the bottom of the line.

I was ecstatic, but the return journey lay ahead of me, and that's always the hardest part. It had taken one minute and 25 seconds to get this far, and it would take at least another 40 seconds to get back. I reached up, toward the lift bag, and unscrewed the valve on the attached tank of compressed air. There was a metal ring around the bottom of the bag, and I pulled the pin, releasing the bag from the weighted half of the sled. Quickly, I grabbed the ring with my left hand and held on for dear life. It's like clinging to the gondola of a balloon as it takes flight. Swoosh! I zoomed toward the surface, 43 stories away.

I rose at a speed of three meters per second, with my lungs still feeling as heavy as wet sponges. At 80 meters, my lungs began to wring themselves out and the blood began returning to my tingling extremities.

At 40 meters, I could see the backlit, transparent ceiling, still high above me. Two minutes had passed.

With 10 meters to go, I reached the most critical part of the dive. I was in the so-called blackout zone. It is during this deadly stretch, in shallow water, with the surface seemingly within easy reach, that free divers most often pass out. The oxygen-starved brain can't take any more and simply shuts down.

But I felt strong, not faint. With five meters left to go, I released the lift bag and let my momentum propel me to the surface. I popped waist-high out of the water, sucked in a breath, clenched my fists, and yelled in triumph. I was back! I heard clapping and shouting; saw the familiar faces of the surface divers; the wildly cheering strangers on the surrounding vessels.

I was spent but fulfilled. I high-fived the surrounding divers and looked around for Audrey. She would be surfacing soon, but she had to do so in stages to give her body time to decompress. I shut my eyes for a second and thanked Olokun. He had seen me through another safe journey.

Then there she was, Audrey, breaking through the surface a few yards to my left. I swam toward her and she pulled the regulator out of her mouth and we kissed.

"I love you," I said.

She wrapped her arms around my neck. "I love you more," she said.

When it was all over, after we had packed up the boat and done our interviews, we went back to the hotel to shower and shave and celebrate with the crew, and, by midnight, Audrey and I were fast asleep, entwined in each other's arms.

Later that morning, we returned to La Paz to fetch Audrey's belongings, then drove to the airport for the flight to Miami.

"Here you are, arriving in Florida with just the clothes on your back," I said, grinning at her as we walked through the terminal. "You came with nothing, just like me."

"No," she replied, smiling. "I came with you."

Life doesn't always place you where or with whom you expect, and I had certainly never expected anyone like Audrey. She was so much younger than me, but in many ways so much wiser. She calmed me down. Centered me. In the space of a week, I felt transformed. Audrey had managed to send the angry Pipín packing. I was a new me.

We were still in the process of settling down in my Miami Beach apartment when Azcarraga called and told me he wanted me to fly out to Los Angeles to meet Alfonso Arau, the Mexican film director. Arau had made a name for himself with *Like Water for Chocolate* and, more recently, *A Walk in the Clouds,* and the studios were chasing him to do American-style movies. Azcarraga had told Arau my story during a lengthy telephone conversation, and Arau had been intrigued enough to ask for a meeting.

I liked him right away. He was a decent, unassuming guy, and a good listener. We went to dinner and talked well into the night, but Arau seemed more interested in hearing stories about Azcarraga—El Tigre—a man he'd never met, than in listening to my own small adventures. I told him the little I knew, and we eventually got back to me, and when Arau heard the story about the Russian submarine—well, his whole demeanor changed. It was as if he'd been waiting for that one story the whole night.

"That right there is the first scene in the movie," he said excitedly. "You're in the waters off the coast of Cuba, spearfishing; you hear this high-pitched whirring behind you. It gets louder and louder. You turn around and find yourself face-to-face with a Russian sub. It's absolutely marvelous!"

When I got back to Miami, Azcarraga called to see how it had gone. I told him it had gone very well and that Arau was going to take a few weeks to think about it before putting pen to paper. "Meanwhile," I said. "I have an idea for a television series. I'm calling it *Planet Ocean*. Each segment focuses on a different sea creature, and each week we find ourselves in an entirely different part of the planet."

"Pipín," Azcarraga said, laughing. "Don't you have enough on your plate already?"

"It's never enough," I said.

The next day I discovered that El Tigre, true to his word, had wired $25,000 into my account, a first installment on the book.

"I can't believe it," I told Audrey.

"Why not?"

"Because most people are all talk. Most people never come through for you."

"We should celebrate," she said.

"We will," I said. "I promise you one thing, Audrey. You will never be bored with me. Our life together is going to be one adventure after another."

Two weeks later, we flew to the island of Roatán, in Honduras, to shoot a film with my friend Solino, and we found ourselves free diving with two bottlenose dolphins that lived in a huge, penned-in cove. Copan, the male, and Maya, the female, occasionally swam with tourists, and I didn't know how I felt about this. I had heard a number of disturbing stories about dolphins in captivity, and one in particular had left its mark on me. It concerned a dolphin that became so distraught in his concrete tank, and so bewildered by his failed attempts at communicating, via sonar, with other dolphins, that he eventually committed suicide by ramming his head into a wall. But in Roatán, these two had room to roam, and Audrey and I found the experience to be truly magical. Copan and Maya were as uninhibited as well-loved children, though not immediately.

The first two days we took it slowly, wanting to give the dolphins a chance to get used to us. The plan was to train them to accompany me on a hundred-meter free dive. It wouldn't be much of a dive for *them:* dolphins can reach depths of more than four hundred meters, and can remain submerged for as long as eight minutes. But for me it was quite a challenge: I had to get there, and *back,* so I would be dependent on their good will.

Initially, neither Copan nor Maya seemed to like me. I was so busy trying to get them to respond to a number of familiar hand signals— signals they'd been taught by their original trainers—that they simply ignored me. Audrey was much more patient. She let both dolphins dominate the interaction, and they responded well. But every time I approached they moved off and took refuge behind Audrey.

At one point, we dropped a cable, put the sled in the water, and I went for a short dive. I was trying to give the dolphins an idea of what I hoped to accomplish. It didn't work. They weren't interested in the sled, and they were less interested in me.

Solino, who was handling one of the cameras, was practically laughing at me. He could see how frustrated I was. But he got some great footage of Audrey and Copan, swimming side by side, inches from each other, practically dancing, and at several points Copan peeled away and twirled around her, stopping long enough to make direct eye contact.

When we took a break on the dock, I was frustrated—and a little jealous. "This isn't going to happen if they refuse to work with me," I said.

"Be patient," Audrey said. "They'll get comfortable with you. Give them time."

The next day, we tried again, with and without the sled, but they didn't respond well to me and even less well to the clanking contraption. I was getting seriously frustrated, and had little appetite for dinner. But later that night Audrey led me down to the water. "We're going to go in," she said, "and I don't want you to do anything. Just lie there, floating on your back, and look at the stars."

It was a clear, crisp night, and the sky was ablaze with stars, and having Audrey floating next to me, holding my hand, made it easy to relax. Before long, the dolphins began circling us, clicking and whistling and blowing air through their nasal passages. This is how they communicate, and how they navigate: dolphins are like living sonars. They can emit twelve hundred sounds per second, and the reverberations guide them through the water.

Suddenly Copan stuck his head out and splashed my chest. I laughed and he let out a high-pitched squeak.

"See?" Audrey said. "You guys just needed to fool around a little."

The next day, Copan and Maya let me hold on to their fins for a short, warm-up dive, but Maya swam off to inspect a cameraman's light, and we had to start again. I could see this was going to be tricky. Getting down to one hundred meters wasn't going to be too difficult, but I was going to need their help getting back.

Just before Audrey's dive in
Spain. I'm holding the release
cable, with a safety diver and
spectators in the background.

Audrey was a little worried. "Aren't you afraid?" she asked.

"No," I said. "What's there to be afraid of?"

"You know what I'm afraid of? I'm afraid of the fact that you're not sufficiently afraid."

"With you at my side, I'll never be afraid."

We tried again. At first, having decided I wasn't as unpleasant as they originally suspected, the dolphins just wanted to have fun. And they seemed to like the fact that I could go so deep without scuba tanks, clearly a new experience for them. They invited me to follow them, and I let them lead. They corkscrewed through the water, came at me, swam past and broke the surface and leaped into the air. It was quite a dazzling acrobatic display.

"This is amazing," Audrey said. "This is a dream come true."

"They're just showing off," I shot back, ribbing her. "We're here to work."

Audrey took over one of the cameras, the one she'd learned to use in the waters off Miami, while Solino and another cameraman waited below. I signaled to the dolphins, and this time they responded. Copan came up along one side and Maya glided next to me on the other. When they were close enough, I grabbed one fin in each hand and let them guide me downward. This was very different than riding the sled. For one thing, I was going down head first. For another, my hands weren't free to equalize the pressure in my ears, and I had to force air through my Eustachian tubes by making pulsing motions inside my nasal cavity.

It was also quite a challenge to hang on to their wriggling backs, especially as we went deeper, where we lost the light completely. I was lucky, though: I had my very own pair of seeing-eye dolphins. I hung on and hoped for the best, then at long last I saw the cameraman's light and knew we had reached our mark.

I tugged gently on both fins, hoping they would respond. Copan and Maya turned in perfect unison and made for the surface, clicking away excitedly, as if they were having a conversation. They led me back up, moving fast, and when I was about twenty feet from the surface I let

Practicing a tandem dive in Miami.

ey and I on a tandem dive in Spain, rocketing back to the surface

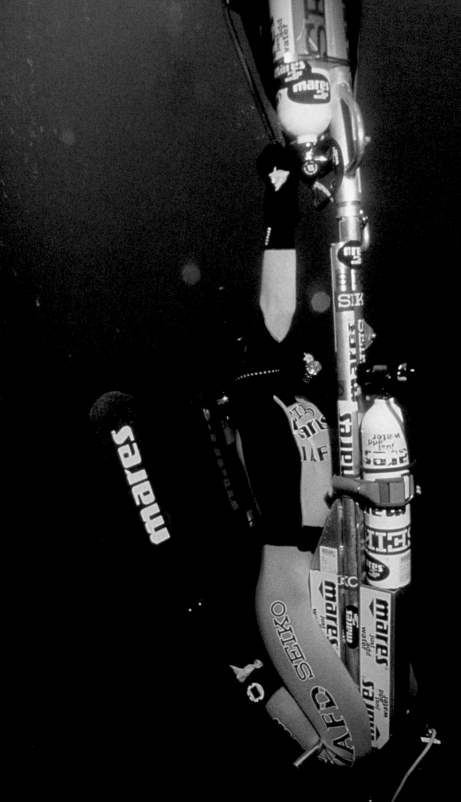
Audrey on her way to setting a record in Spain.

A triumphant kiss after Audrey set her record in Spain.

In Cozumel, preparing to set a record.

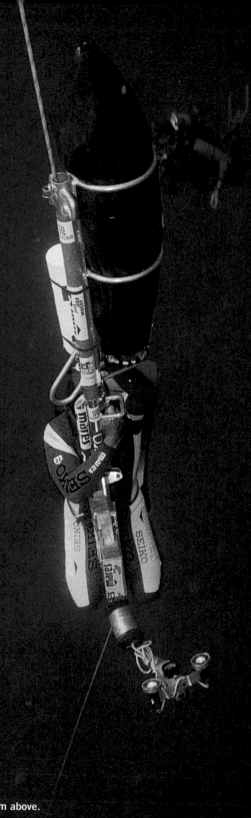

A view of the lift bag from above.

Taking a warm-up dive before the main event.

Audrey in Spain. The cylindrical device on her back is actually a computer designed to track every second of the dive.

Audrey surfacing in a storm of bubbles after a dive in Spain. On the right you can see a safety diver's lights far below Audrey.

Audrey and I meditate in the water before a dive.

Audrey breaking the surface and taking a sweet gulp of air.

Warm-up exercises in Grand Cayman.

Audrey in the Grand Cayman, swimming with a curious manta ray.

Audrey in the Red Sea during the filming of the Mexican TV series.

Exploring was her passion since childhood. In the background a reef is faintly visible.

With that playful manta in Grand Cayman.

Training Audrey in Miami.

As much of a natural as Audrey was, she also worked diligently to improve.

Audrey photographed me meditating underwater in the Bahamas.

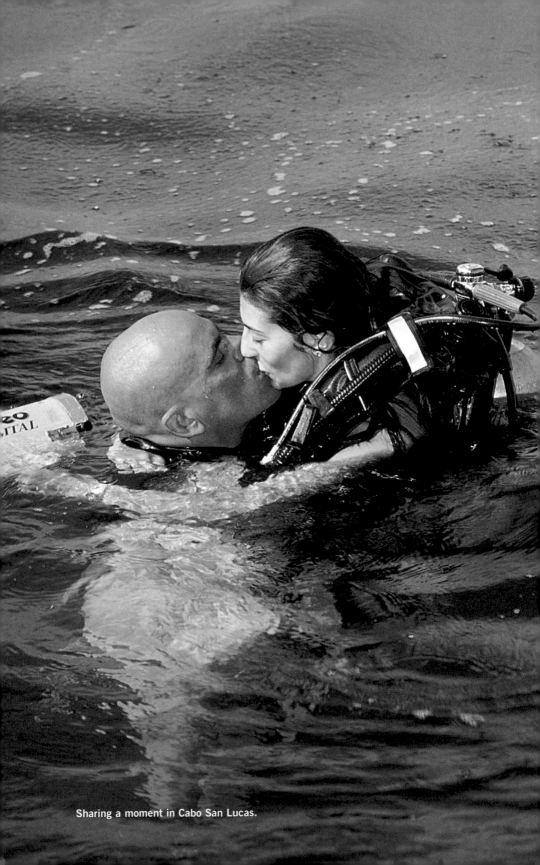

Sharing a moment in Cabo San Lucas.

go. The momentum carried me the rest of the way up, and I surfaced in time to watch them leaping out of the water and arcing through the air.

Audrey's face lit up, but she was crying. I swam to her side, confused. I was still flying—still high on adrenaline.

"What's wrong?" I asked.

"Nothing," she said. "It was beautiful. I don't think I've ever seen anything so magical in my life."

It was hard to say good-bye to our new pals. But we had to get back to Miami. I had a book to write. Part of the advance had paid for the trip to Roatán.

I was thinking about hiring someone to help me get started, but Audrey offered to take care of it. I thought she meant she was going to help me find the right person, but a few days later she put a tape recorder on the table between us and told me to start talking.

"Where do I start?" I said.

"At the beginning. With that little boy who could neither walk nor talk. The one they had to fit with orthopedic shoes."

A few days later, I got another call from Sector. They wanted to continue to sponsor me, and they upped the ante to $75,000 a year. I'm no fool. I asked for annual bumps of $25,000 and accepted the offer. Two weeks later, when the first check arrived, I walked Audrey to my car and told her we had an important meeting to attend.

"Meeting?" she said. "What meeting? With whom?"

"You'll see."

We reached my bank and went inside and I looked for my regular rep. "This is Audrey Mestre," I said. "From now on, she's in charge of all my money. Everything. She runs the show, okay?"

The woman asked if she could have a word with me, privately, and we stepped away from the desk, out of earshot. "Pipín," she said. "I don't understand you. The last time I saw you, you came in with Yamile, and you withdrew your last dollar and gave her everything. Now you come in with this very attractive young lady, Miss Mestre, and again you give away all your money."

"I know," I said. "I'm terrible with money. I don't want to go anywhere near it. Audrey's much better than me at everything."

"I don't know, Pipín. Men, women, and money—it's a dangerous combination."

"Not this time. This isn't just any woman. I am going to marry this woman. I am going to have babies with this woman and we're going to grow old together. You watch: I'll be coming by to open college accounts for each of our children."

That night Audrey and I went to dinner with my little boy, Luca. He was always shy when he first saw her, but by the time the food arrived he was in love with her all over again. And why not? He couldn't have asked for a better stepmom.

Everything in my life was going beautifully. The world seemed alive with possibilities.

A couple of months later, while Audrey and I were balancing two jobs—working on the book and editing the footage we'd shot in Roatán—I got news from Italy: Umberto Pelizzari had just broken my No Limits record with a dive of 131 meters.

At the end of the week, I announced that I would recapture the crown, and that I intended to do it in Cabo, site of my most recent success. I hammed it up for the press. I told them that the Italian would never beat me, and that no matter how deep he tried to go I would always shoot past him like a bullet, leaving him in my turbulent wake.

"How deep is deep enough?" Audrey asked me on the way home from the press conference. She seemed worried.

"I don't know," I said. "That's impossible to answer."

"There's a limit to this, Pipín," she said. "There's a point of no return."

"You're wrong," I said. "That's why it's called No Limits."

A few weeks later, Audrey and I were on a plane to Cabo. I took her hand as we came in for a landing.

"I feel like we're on our honeymoon," I said. "Going back to the place we met."

"Really?" she said. "I feel like I've been on my honeymoon since we met."

"You mean that?"

"Yes, you big lug," she said, giving me a quick kiss on the lips. "Why is that so hard to believe?"

"I don't know," I said. "I'm still trying to figure out what I've done to deserve you."

"Somebody up there must like you," she said, her eyes sparkling.

"Somebody *down* there," I said. "Olokun, god of the ocean."

But Olokun wasn't in a good mood that week. Pepe Fernández flew in from Cuba to supervise the crew, and Kim McCoy flew in from San Diego, with his computers, and everything started to go wrong from the start.

The first mishap occurred almost as soon as we arrived. We showed up at the house we'd rented and a scorpion bit Pepe on the foot. He howled in pain and collapsed on the couch. He said it felt as if someone had hammered a stake into his arch. Pepe was a solidly built guy, with hands the size of a catcher's mitt, and frankly it was a bit of a shock to hear him cry. We put ice on the wound and gave him a double dose of aspirin, and he eventually fell sleep.

The next morning, Pepe assured us he was feeling fine, and we went out to the bay to drop the anchor. We tried attaching it to a marker buoy, so that we could keep the boat moored there, but the damn thing kept getting pulled below the surface by the weight of the unwieldy anchor. It took hours to set it properly, at which point we were all exhausted and in a bad mood. It felt like a harbinger of things to come.

We didn't have time to mope, however. It was time for my practice dive. I planned to go to eighty meters, and Pepe was supposed to be my safety diver, but his foot was still swollen and he didn't look so hot.

"Are you sure you want to do this?" I asked him.

"I can do it, man. I'm fine. Relax."

Audrey on the beach in Miami.

When the time came, Pepe and the other safety divers slipped into the water, and someone on the boat counted down, then I did my dive and surfaced. It was uneventful, which was a good thing.

We all waited for Pepe to make his way up the decompression line, but after a few minutes I started to get nervous. I don't know why; I just felt something was wrong. I jumped in, looking for him, and by the time I swam back I saw him floating on the surface, unconscious. We whisked him to shore on the skiff, and we tried to revive him en route, but by the time we reached land he was gone.

I was stunned. For the second time in eight months, one of my safety divers had died under baffling circumstances, and this time he had been a dear friend, someone I'd known for years—someone whose wife and daughter I'd spent time with. *The man who had introduced me to Audrey.*

Pepe and I had some real history together, and now he was dead, and I couldn't for the life of me understand what had gone wrong. He was an experienced diver. Had he come up too fast? Had he blacked out? Had he suffered some kind of embolism?

When the report came back from the coroner's office, the official cause of death was listed as drowning. But one of the paramedics on the scene speculated that the scorpion bite may have played a pivotal role. "It's possible that the poison reacted to the nitrogen from the compressed air," he suggested. "It could have been forced into his bloodstream at high pressure."

I guess his theory was as good as any, but the fact is that none of us would ever know, and not knowing made us feel that much more powerless and confused. I was so depressed that I decided to cancel the dive.

"Are you sure you want to cancel?" Audrey asked me.

"No," I said. "I'm not sure about anything anymore."

"Pipín," she said. "I'm not going to try to sway you, one way or the other, but you've been through this before. This is the life you've chosen. These things happen."

I was really confused. I thought it would be insensitive to make the dive, but at the same time I wondered if Pepe would have wanted me to see it through. "I feel like I should do it," I said, breaking the silence. "For him. But I also feel like I'm trying to justify it to myself."

"You don't have to justify anything," Audrey said. "It was an accident. I'm not going to sit here and allow you to blame yourself."

I was amazed by Audrey's equanimity. Just having her in the room, next to me, went a long way toward calming me down. It struck me that to leave Cabo now, without making the dive, might make everything seem even more hopeless. And I realized that I really should make the dive in honor of my good friend.

"Do you think I'm making the right decision?" I asked Audrey.

"Do you?"

"Yes."

"Then that's what matters, isn't it? But if it's any consolation, I think it's absolutely the right decision, and I'm behind you one hundred percent."

I phoned Kim McCoy and told him that I wanted to go through with the dive, and the next day I was back in the water. I started with two practice dives, then we set the cable at the 133-meter mark. If I made it, I'd reclaim the crown, and I'd be doing it for both Pepe and myself.

But it was turning into a very windy day, and the current in the bay was unusually strong that day. Kim advised me to postpone the dive, but I didn't want to have to start again from scratch.

"Let's just do it," I said.

"I don't like it," Kim said. "The conditions are very unstable."

I didn't listen. I swam across the choppy water and held on to the sled. The waves were high; they kept slapping me in the face. The boat was rocking back and forth in the choppy surf.

I nodded and the safety divers plunged in. We waited, counting down, and when the countdown ended I pulled the release cord and plummeted into the water.

Within seconds, Kim noticed that the catamaran was moving. There were several spectator boats tied to it, and the collective weight, along with the high wind and the strong current, had managed to pull the anchor loose. Kim scrambled off to see the skipper, to determine how far we had drifted, and he was stunned to discover that there was no Global Positioning System on board.

Meanwhile, I was speeding toward catastrophe. The end of the cable had caught on an underwater spire, and the sled was on a collision course with the ledge of a wall of rock. One of the safety divers realized we were moving out of position, and he tried to warn me, but my eyes were tightly closed and I simply shot past.

Suddenly there was a horrible, ugly crunching noise—metal scraping against rock—and a second safety diver managed to yank me off the sled just seconds before it slammed full force into the ledge. I opened my eyes, completely disoriented, and tried to figure out what had just happened, then reached for the lift bag and found it jammed. The diver offered me his regulator, but I refused. I didn't want to stay in the water for hours, decompressing; I honestly thought I could swim to the top. But within half a minute it was clear I wasn't going to make it to the surface, and two other divers swooped in to give me air.

I stayed below with them, buddy-breathing, and we slowly worked our way to the top, making several decompression stops en route.

I got out of the water in a horribly foul mood. Everything had gone wrong. The fans were disappointed. The reporters and cameramen were disappointed. I was disappointed.

For the next thirty-six hours, while the crew repaired the badly damaged sled, I was a monster. Even Audrey couldn't approach me, nor did she want to. She had never seen this side of me.

But late on the second day I came out of my funk. "I'm sorry I've been such an ogre," I told Audrey.

"That's okay," she said. "I love you anyway."

I needed to hear that. I was going to try again at noon that day, but I was still in a pretty grim mood. I missed Pepe fiercely. I had wanted to make the dive in his honor, and everything had turned to shit.

I don't even remember how I got out to the site. I was like a zombie that day, probably not an ideal state of mind for diving. But I got in the water, prepared myself, and vaguely remember seeing the safety divers disappearing below the surface to take up their positions.

Then—boom!—I was on my way.

I made it—133 meters; the crown was mine again—and surfaced to the usual, raucous cheers. I waved and smiled dutifully for the fans and the cameras, but inside I was feeling empty and lost, and the dark clouds didn't part until we were back in Miami.

Victory had never tasted less sweet.

A practice dive in placid water.

↓

Chapter_ SIX:

PUSHING
THE LIMITS

In Spain, the year Audrey set
her record. Here we're practicing
a tandem dive together.

Once home, I tried to take my mind off the trip by focusing on the book and on the video. But there were other, more mundane matters to attend to. For one thing, I was still living like a bachelor. The bedroom of my tiny South Beach apartment also doubled as an office, and it was cluttered with video equipment and diving gear. And the living room, equally chaotic, had become Jorge Solino's home away from home: he and his wife had split up *again,* and this time it looked like it was going to be permanent.

Audrey did her best to make order, and one day, while struggling to make room in one of the tiny closets, she came across a blouse that clearly didn't belong to her.

"Is this Yamile's?" she said.

"Uh, no," I said. I didn't want to lie to her.

She tossed the blouse into a corner and kept making order, completely unfazed.

"You're not going to get mad?" I said.

"No," she replied.

"Wow. I expected you to go into a jealous rage."

"It's not worth it," she said, smiling like an imp. "And why bother? Whoever she was, she had terrible fashion sense."

I was astonished by Audrey, but there was more to come: "You know what, Pipín?" she said over dinner a few nights later. "It's time to buy a house."

"That would be nice," I said, "*pero con que culo se sienta la cucaracha?*" That's a Cuban expression. It means, "How does a cockroach sit down if it doesn't have an ass?"

"We have enough money for a decent down payment," Audrey said. "Trust me."

"Okay," I said. "You're the boss. If you think we can swing a house, let's look for a house."

Solino shook his head in amazement. "*Coño.* You two. You move *fast.*"

"When it's right, it's right," I said.

"Audrey," he added, turning to face her, "you have more power over this man than Olokun."

Then it struck me: I hadn't been paying much attention to Olokun since we'd returned from Cabo, probably because I was still pissed at him. But I wanted that temperamental god on our side. So I went over to the corner of the living room and lit a candle next to his ceramic bowl, and I tossed in some honey and a broken seashell and a few herbs and did my little song and dance.

When I was done, Audrey wanted to know what I had asked for. "A house on the water," I said.

"Good luck," Solino said, laughing, and he went off to work on the video.

The following Sunday, we began house hunting. I really did want a place on the water, somewhere to dock the boat I didn't own yet, but Olokun wasn't coming through for us. After hours of looking at a bunch of places that were way out of our price range, I turned toward home. But as we were cruising past North Bay Village, a town of man-made islands perched between Miami and Miami Beach, and connected by the Seventy-ninth Street Causeway, we saw yet another sign for an open house.

Audrey and I looked at each other. It was worth a shot. The area had once been known for its Mafia-run strip clubs, but lately it was said to be "in transition." To most people, that euphemism made the area seem instantly undesirable. But to me, it meant there was hope—it meant we might actually find something we could afford.

We followed the signs to Treasure Island and arrived at the house just as the realtor, a young Argentinian, and the owner, a middle-aged local, were getting ready to leave.

"Is it too late?" Audrey asked.

"No," the realtor said. "Not at all. Come on in."

The realtor unlocked the front door and ushered us through, and the moment we stepped inside we both knew that this was it. Beyond the spacious living area, we could see a big dock, and beyond that, the Intracoastal Waterway. Audrey and I didn't want to betray our excitement. *Okay. All right. Fine. Keep cool. Wouldn't want them to jack up the price.*

We took a little tour, trying to act nonchalant. Three bedrooms, a nice kitchen, plenty of closets, and some nice built-ins here and there. But, most of all, that dock. We stepped through a rear door to the lovely sound of water slapping against pylons. We could see the bay and downtown Miami, and the setting sun had turned the sky flamingo-pink.

We went back inside. "I think we might be sort of interested," I said. "What are you asking?"

"Three fifty," the realtor said.

Audrey and I went out to the dock to discuss it in private. She had already spoken to the bank, and they were ready to approve a $400,000 loan, but I felt we could do better. I went in and offered them two eighty. "That's the best I can do," I said. "Take it or leave it."

"Sorry," the owner said.

"Well, thanks for your time," I said. "Here's my number, in case you change your mind."

I took Audrey by the hand and we left, and my cell phone rang before we'd gone two blocks. It was the realtor.

"Why don't you come back?" he said. "Let's talk about this. We're all reasonable people, right?"

I turned around and went back and parked and the realtor was waiting for us by the open front door. He smiled pleasantly and showed us inside again. The owner said he was willing to lower the price to $325,000, and not a penny less. I offered him two ninety.

"Impossible," he said. "The place is worth three forty."

We left and got back in the car and this time we'd gone *three* blocks before the phone rang. It was the realtor again. "Okay," he said. "You win. You can have it for two ninety."

Audrey's parents flew in to have a look at the house, since we valued their opinion. They loved it as much as we did, and we signed on the dotted line and went out to celebrate. I was a happy man. I'd fallen in love with Audrey and inherited a terrific family.

Three months later, we moved in. We had a home, a *real* home, right on the water.

"America's been berry berry good to me!" I joked.

Audrey laughed. "I can't believe we did it," she said. "I almost feel like an adult."

We got a good price on a "slightly damaged" forty-one-foot fishing boat, which I had to refurbish and convert into a diving boat. I still remember pulling up to the dock, and cutting the engine, and getting out. And I remember turning to look at it, *our* boat, moored at *our* dock. I was overwhelmed. America *had* been very good to me. The unbelievable woman next to me. The water lapping at the pylons underfoot. The city, gleaming in the near distance. Not all that long ago, I'd arrived in Miami with practically nothing, and here I was with a home and a yacht and a gorgeous woman who made it all *mean* something.

We named the boat *Olokun.*

Having a home changed me. I felt ready for the next chapter in my life. And with Audrey, as I've said, I felt unstoppable.

Our life revolved around the water. We were working on a book about my early years in Cuba, we hoped to parlay our dolphin adventure in Honduras into a television series, and—last but not least—I was eager to try to turn free diving into an *American* sport.

Back in Europe, free diving still had thousands of devotees, but my old nemesis Pelizzari seemed to be losing interest in No Limits. Like a number of critics, he began to see No Limits as something of a circus act, and he had recently become enamored with the "purity" of Constant Weight. He was drawn to the challenge of diving under his own steam, he said, without the sled. He wouldn't be going to anywhere near the depths he had gone before, of course, but—the way he saw it— the distance he covered would belong to him.

I guess that's as good an argument as any, but I hadn't come to the same conclusion. Both branches of the sport were equally valid. You could even argue that they were two entirely different sports. By this stage in his career, for whatever reason, Pelizzari had lost interest in No Limits. But to me, No Limits was still what it was all about. To push the envelope. To go deeper than any human being had ever gone before.

And, yes—part of the thrill was connected to fear; cutting it close, wondering if you were going to make it back. But isn't that often the case? Why do men bother with Everest? Not because it's there; we all know it's there. They do it for the challenge, to test themselves; and they do it for the thrill.

I was suddenly reminded of the famous trapeze artist Karl Wallenda. Many years ago he said something I have never forgotten: "Being on the wire is living. Everything else is waiting."

Being on the wire was an act, of course. But people were riveted. And part of the appeal came from the fact that Wallenda made his way across the wire without a net. *It's just me and gravity, folks. Me against the elements.*

That's how I felt about free diving. I didn't have a net, either. And there was one other thing I didn't have: an audience. Oh, sure, plenty of people turned out to watch, even here, in the U.S., but the sport remained very much in its infancy, and I wanted to change that. Free diving could not exist in a vacuum, and I could not exist without free diving.

With that in mind, I had begun giving free-diving classes, right there in Miami, and two of my more promising students turned out to be women. One was Amy Castro, a local diver; the other was Meghan Heaney-Grier, of Little Torch Key, Florida. I had met Amy years earlier, and she had gone with me to Buffalo, New York, to help with the experiments at the Center for Research in Extreme Environments. Meghan was a local model who did water-related stunt work for movies and television. I knew her through her friend Mark, who was one of the best underwater cameramen I'd ever worked with.

Audrey riding the sled on her way down.

I began to think that this was exactly what the sport needed: fit, photogenic women in bathing suits, doing incredible things in the water. I know that sounds a little sexist, but you'll have to forgive me: I was learning to think like a capitalist.

Whenever Amy came over to the house to work out, Audrey joined us. We had created an outdoor gym right on the dock—free weights, ab machines, even a Jacuzzi—and we were getting into the best physical shape of our lives. We were also learning how to breathe properly, which is of course the key to the sport, and practicing Pranayama yoga became part of our lives. Pranayama is all about relaxing the mind and body, which is done largely through proper breathing techniques. I had been practicing since my days in Cuba, but I didn't know it had a name back then—I didn't know it had a name until Jacques Mayol had uttered it— so in effect I was doing yoga by default. By now it had become part of my daily life, and its usefulness went beyond breathing techniques: yoga helped center me.

Once or twice a week, we would take the boat out and go free diving, and Audrey would come along, with her tanks. But pretty soon she was joining us without them, and I was impressed by how quickly she took to the sport. I had seen her in the water in Roatán, swimming with the dolphins, without tanks, but that had been recreational, and this was more serious, more focused.

One evening, while we were relaxing in the Jacuzzi after a six-mile run, Audrey told me she wanted to show me something.

"What?"

"You'll see," she said. "And get ready to time me."

She took a series of deep breaths, using the Pranayama techniques, then dunked her head in the bubbling water. I clicked my watch. I figured she might be able to do three minutes, four maximum, but she kept going. To my amazement, she didn't come up for air for more than five minutes.

"What do you think?" she said after she managed to catch her breath.

"I'm in shock," I said.

"Really?"

I really was. I thought she had probably come very close to setting the women's world record for static apnea, or breath-holding, and I told her so.

"I'm not interested in records," she said, smiling coyly. "I just did it to impress you."

"Well, I'm impressed."

For the next few days, I could think of little else. I was training two other women, but I had a potential champ under my own roof. A few nights later, I finally told Audrey what I was thinking—that she could become a free-diving champ, and that we could become free-diving champs together.

"I don't think I'm interested," she said.

"Why not?"

"I don't know. One record holder in the family is enough. And I enjoy being a safety diver. I get more of a thrill from just watching you do what you do."

The next day, I went spearfishing, and Audrey came along to keep me company. When we'd caught enough grouper for a month's worth of dinners, I left the spear gun in the boat and we horsed around in the water. Audrey followed me to a depth of twenty-five meters, and it took no apparent effort whatsoever. When we came up for air, I couldn't help but tell her again. "You're a natural. Give me six months and I'll turn you into the women's free-diving champ."

"I'm not interested in records," she repeated. "I don't have a competitive bone in my body." We swam back to the boat. "On the other hand," she added. "It *is* fun."

And that was it. That was the turning point. Audrey decided she wouldn't mind giving the sport a try, but not for anyone but herself.

"Then you've got the right attitude," I said. "That's what the sport's about. It's about being the best you can be."

She smiled that coy smile of hers again.

"What?" I said, curious.

"Maybe I lied a little."

"About what?"

"I have another reason for free diving."

"Yeah?"

"Sometimes, I wonder what it is that goes on down there. In your mind, I mean. I wonder what you're thinking and feeling. And I guess I feel that if I know, well—it might bring us even closer together."

I didn't think we could be any closer, and I told her so. I had never been as close to anyone in my entire life. I hadn't known that this level of closeness *existed*. But once again Audrey proved me wrong. When we began free diving together, it was as if we had entered another dimension—a dimension in which there were truly No Limits.

Audrey took her training very seriously. She didn't do anything by half-measures. And she was doing it not for herself, but for us. Much later, in response to a fan's question, she wrote on her website: "It is very difficult to live with someone who experiences sensations unknown by the rest of the world, sensations that can't be described or shared. I thought if I could enter [Pipín's] underwater world I could be closer to him."

Audrey had given me a gift. She was trying to connect with me on a level that was probably beyond human comprehension. What makes a man wrap himself around a weighted sled and plunge hundreds of feet into the ocean? And what happens to him at those depths—physically, mentally, spiritually?

Jacques Mayol used to say that entering the water for a free dive was like making love to the ocean. And, indeed, the sea has often been described as a seductive siren, luring men into its often dangerous embrace. That was a lot to compete with, and Audrey was wise enough to steer clear of competition. She had decided to become part of it instead.

Audrey trained three or four hours per day, come hell or high water. She had spent many years in a back brace, and was finely attuned to her own body. She took care of it and listened to it and responded to its needs. She was impressively disciplined, both physically and mentally.

We went to Grand Cayman in May 1997. I had been curious about the possibility of a two-breath dive, meaning that I would stop at some point on my way down, take a generous hit of air from one of my safety divers, and keep going. I wanted to know how far I could go, as usual, and I wanted to know if there would be any physiological ill effects. Before we left, Audrey and I had decided that this would be a good time for her to try for a first record, something she could begin to build on.

Unfortunately, the trip began with a setback. After an eighty-meter practice dive, I went back into the water and descended on scuba to recover the sled. When I returned to the boat, I lapsed into convulsions and fainted. I had stayed too deep for too long, ascended too quickly, and now found myself felled by decompression sickness, the so-called bends. This is one of the greatest dangers of diving. I've had it—in varying degrees of seriousness—more times than I can count.

The bends have a long and frightening history. The first written account goes back to the nineteenth century, to the French tunnel builders of the era. The men worked in dry chambers—known as *caissons*, French for "big boxes"—that were pumped full of air. Many of them suffered dizzy spells, acute pain in the joints or abdomen, itching, rashes, and even a bluish discoloration of the skin. As the excavations went ever deeper, some of the men would be stricken by excruciating pain, and would double over and die. The men were understandably terrified by this mysterious ailment. They came to know it as caisson disease. Years later, in America, during construction of the Brooklyn Bridge, the men noted the double-over posture of the stricken laborers and began referring to the ailment as "the bends."

It wasn't until 1878 that French physiologist Paul Bert finally discovered the cause. Ordinarily, we breathe a mixture of air that is four-fifths nitrogen and one-fifth oxygen. When nitrogen is dissolved in the body at sea level, it is harmless. But at deeper levels more and more is absorbed into the blood and tissues. If, for example, you triple the pressure on your body, you also triple the amount of nitrogen that becomes dissolved in the body. And if you relieve that pressure too abruptly, the gas tends to form bubbles in the blood. Think of the body as a can of soda pop that's been shaken. When you pull the top, the pressure is suddenly reduced, and it fizzes and spills over. Well, the nitrogen in the body works very much in the same manner. And it can find its way into your blood, joints, spine, and even brain. A diver can become blinded, paralyzed, or asphyxiated by the bends. Embolisms are not uncommon, and neither are blackouts and convulsions.

Lesser symptoms might include a bumpy rash, or discoloration of the skin. And the attendant pain—in the shoulders, knees, hips, elbows—can range from an excruciating cramp to a dull ache. Sometimes you feel as if there's something tunneling inside your skin that just won't quit, and it can drive you absolutely crazy.

With the exception of blackouts, which occur for wholly different reasons, free divers don't have to contend with most of these symptoms. That's because we're not breathing air from a tank—we're not breathing, period. So there's no need to decompress. But when you're wearing tanks, you have to return to the surface slowly, giving the nitrogen enough time to get out of the bloodstream. The bubbles won't form if the pressure is relieved gradually. And there's a right way to do it. Decompression isn't guesswork; it's science.

To this day, both recreational and professional divers depend on the so-called decompression tables. The first of these date back to 1907, when J. S. Haldane, a British physiologist, began conducting experiments on Royal Navy divers. He determined that a number of stops were required on the ascent to get the nitrogen out of one's system, and he had mathematically prescribed "waiting stages" depending on the depth of the dive.

A diver who spends 30 minutes at 190 feet, for example, must stop and decompress for one minute when he's 40 feet from the surface, another 8 minutes at 30 feet, an additional 19 minutes at 20 feet, and, finally, 43 more minutes at 10 feet. The general guideline on the ascent rate is 60 feet per minute. One must never ascend faster than the exhaled bubbles, and one must take a healthy break between dives.

If a diver does show signs of decompression sickness, he can go back down, recompress, and repeat his ascent according to the tables. But the most effective treatment is to be placed in a recompression or hyperbaric chamber, which duplicates the conditions underwater. The diver waits inside and, as the pressure on his body is decreased, the nitrogen seeps out of his blood and tissues.

During that dive in the Caymans, as soon as I became unconscious, I was immediately rushed to the only hyperbaric chamber on the island. But I regained consciousness before we reached the chamber, and I got into a screaming argument with the doctor. The problem is that I'm hypersensitive to pure oxygen, and in the chamber you're breathing pure oxygen at two or three atmospheres of pressure. That was the last place I wanted to be.

"You are not putting me in there!" I shouted. "I was in one of those things in Cuba once and started having seizures."

"The longer you wait, the worse it's going to get," the doctor said.

I didn't see it that way. This was one case where the cure seemed worse than the disease. "Let me go back to the water to decompress properly," I suggested. "That's what I've always done in the past. You can't force me into that damn thing!"

I was really screaming by now, and not even Audrey could calm me down.

"Pipín, we have no choice," she said, pleading with me. "You've got to get in there."

That's the last thing I remember. I found out later that they pumped me full of sedatives and had me airlifted to South Miami Hospital. The doctors there were very concerned. They warned Audrey that if a bubble blocked circulation, I could be brain-damaged or paralyzed. I was unconscious for three days. When I woke up, Audrey was sitting next to my bed.

"What am I doing here?" I said. I was completely disoriented. I was laid out like an old man, with wires everywhere, an IV in my left arm, and monitoring machines against the wall, blipping and bleating away. "What the hell is going on?"

Audrey was so relieved to see me awake that it was a few moments before she could even talk. "You—you've been out for three days," she said at last. "I've never been so scared in my life."

"Three days?" I said, aghast. I couldn't get my mind around the fact that this had happened to *me*.

"Yes," Audrey said. "It was terrifying. And the doctors didn't help. They scared me half to death."

"That's what they're good at," I said. "Now come on, help me get the hell out of here."

"Pipín—"

Before she could protest further, I ripped the IV out of my arm and pushed the wires aside and got to my feet. I felt light-headed and dizzy and Audrey had to support me until the feeling passed.

"Jesus, what is wrong with me!"

"Pipín, please. I'm asking you nicely: get back into bed."

"No, I refuse to stay in this place another minute," I said. "I'm sorry."

Reluctantly, Audrey helped me down the corridor, and into the elevator, and out to the parking area. I could feel my hospital gown flapping in the breeze, and I knew my bare ass was winking at passers-by. I can't imagine it was a pretty sight, though part of me would like to think otherwise.

Once we got home, I went and did my song and dance for Olokun, thanked him for sparing me, and rejoined Audrey on the dock.

"I want to go back to the Caymans tomorrow," I said.

"I think we should wait a while."

"Okay. We'll wait till Saturday."

I went back inside and grabbed the phone and called the representative I'd been dealing with at the Caymans' ministry of tourism. "I'll be back this weekend," I said.

"I don't think so," he said. "We're not interested."

I told him they should get interested or I'd sue. "I'm stuck with a massive medical bill because *your* doctor was incompetent," I said. I can be a real asshole when the situation calls for it. Sometimes I can be an asshole when the situation doesn't call for it.

"Okay," the guy said. "Let me know when you're coming."

We flew back to Grand Cayman at the end of May, but there seemed to be little enthusiasm for my "Cayman Challenge." One reporter dismissed the whole thing as a freak show. And even a number of free-diving aficionados had serious questions about the planned event. What was the point of pausing for a hit of oxygen at the halfway mark, they asked, when the idea had always been to make the trip on a *single* breath of air? I'm just as much of a purist as the next guy, and I understood their criticism, but this was different. I wanted to try something new. No one had ever been anywhere near a depth of 150 meters, and I wanted to see how the human body would respond. *My* body.

I also wanted to prove a point. I had done something like this many years earlier, in Cuba, but at much shallower depths. Very early in my career, one of my friends and I had come across an antique Soviet scuba tank, and we had set it on a ledge, some 30 meters down, and gone back from time to time to take hits of oxygen so we could stay down longer and continue fishing. We had done that in the name of efficiency. This event was for science.

Alas, even my hero Jacques Mayol didn't think much of the idea. Like everyone else, he predicted I'd rip a hole in my compressed lungs by taking air from a regulator at that depth. I ran a very high risk of an embolism, he said.

But how could any of them be so sure? No one had ever tried it. No one really knew what might happen beyond 120 meters. The vast majority of free divers believed that to breathe from a tank at any point beyond 75 meters was too dangerous. Most of them said they'd rather gamble on getting to the surface without air than take oxygen from a safety diver.

"He won't make it," they said. "It's impossible."

Their lack of faith only made me more determined to prove them wrong. I was going to go ahead with my experiment. I wasn't interested in speculation. I wanted to know what would really happen at those depths.

Audrey was on the fence, but she didn't want to stand in my way.

On the appointed day, with Audrey and four other safety divers in the water, I rode the sled down to the 75-meter mark and took a breath from a spare tank that was tied to the line. Then I continued my journey, stopped the sled at exactly 150 meters, inflated the lift bag, and rocketed back to the surface.

My body was literally propelled out of the water. I felt great. I punched the air with my fist. I think I even shouted with glee. I felt I was making history and making good science. I had taken my body to unheard-of depths—the length of two city blocks—and I had returned unscathed. Maybe I could do it on one breath someday . . .

It was nice to see that the mood on the boat had changed. Even the biggest doubters came by to shake my hand and offer their congratulations. But oddly enough, I wasn't even processing their good wishes and kind words. I was only thinking about the future.

"Can you imagine what I might be capable of someday?" I said.

"No," she said, and she smiled a patronizing little smile.

"Oh, I get it," I said. "I sound like an egomaniac."

"Yes, you do," she said, still smiling. "But that's the way it is. Sometimes you have to believe in yourself to a point of lunacy."

"I think you've been here before," I said.

"The Caymans?" she replied, confused. "Uh—I don't think so, Pipín. What are you talking about?"

"Not the Caymans," I said. "Planet Earth. I think you've lived other lives before this one. You're too wise for someone your age."

"Maybe I was a mermaid in one of those lives," she said. "And I did something wrong. And my bad karma brought me back as a human being."

"So you think this is a punishment?"

"Being a person is definitely a step down from mermaid," she said. "But being with you makes it bearable."

That Audrey. She was amazing.

We had a couple of days before Audrey's dive. We were planning on doing a Constant Weight dive, something fairly demanding—maybe sixty meters. But while we were fooling around in the water the next day, she asked if she could give the sled a try.

She hopped aboard and braced herself and I pulled the decoupling pin and sent her on her way, but she stopped after only twenty-five meters, inflated the lift bag, and popped back up.

"Wow," she said. "That was weird."

"Good weird or bad weird?"

"Awesome weird."

"So why did you stop so soon?"

"Did I?"

"Yes," I said. "You only went down to twenty-five meters."

"I don't have a good feel for it yet," she said. "It's very disorienting. It's such a rush and I was moving so fast that I thought I'd overshot the mark."

She was right on all counts. At first, it *is* very disorienting. You do think you're moving too fast, and you worry that you've gone too far. But once you get the hang of the sled, it's as easy as riding a bike.

We practiced for two days. She loved it.

"You look like you're high," I said.

"I *feel* like I'm high," she said, beaming.

"It's amazing, isn't it?"

"Beyond amazing," she said.

"Just think: if Jacques Mayol and Enzo Maiorca had been satisfied to swim within the limits, we wouldn't be here. But those crazy bastards wanted to go deeper. They're the ones that came up with this whole crazy concept—riding a weighted sled along a cable and smashing all barriers."

147

"What a rush," she said.

"You're beginning to understand," I said, kissing her.

"Yes, I am," she said, grinning to beat the band.

It suddenly occurred to me that Audrey should forget about the Constant Weight record. We were about No Limits, so there wasn't much point in bothering with Constant Weight.

"You think I can do it?" she asked.

"I know you can do it."

We practiced for two more days. On the big day, she popped down to eighty meters and flew back up like it was nothing. She was crying when she surfaced, but they were tears of joy.

"Oh, my God," she moaned.

"Cut that out," I said, laughing. "You sound like you do in bed."

"I *feel* like that," she said.

"Now you know," I said.

She reached over and dunked my bald head under water, still laughing. I was more in love than ever.

"Do you know that it took Enzo Maiorca thirteen years to reach eighty meters?" I asked her over a celebratory dinner that night. There was a candle on the restaurant table. She was glowing.

"I felt like I was entering another dimension," she said.

"You're hooked," I said.

"You're right," she said. "I am."

When we got back to Miami, I tried to inject some life into the International Association of Free Divers (IAFD), a fledgling organization I had founded some months earlier. I had initially set it up as the marketing and teaching arm of my filmmaking company, Pipín Productions, but I was suddenly interested in doing more with it. There was another organization called the International Association for the Development of Apnea (IADA), based in Switzerland, which responsible for sanctioning and verifying breath-hold dives around the world. It is a huge, nonprofit, international federation. It has a board of directors, is recognized in more than thirty countries, and holds annual competitions in nine disciplines, exercising a virtual monopoly over the sport. All the recognized free divers—Pelizzari, Frenchman Loïc Leferme, Germany's Benjamin Franz, Czech Martin Stepanek, Tanya Streeter of the Cayman Islands—were aligned with IADA, and in fact Pelizzari was one of the founding members. I, on the other hand, was not an IADA darling. For one thing, I had come up with the whole concept of No Limits, and with the idea of riding the sled in an upright position, and they never acknowledged these critical contributions to the sport. For another, they were jealous: I was a kid from Cuba, and I was breaking records every few months, and they felt this was a European sport, with a fifty-year tradition in Europe. They saw me as a brash, young upstart. We also battled over their requirements. They felt they couldn't verify a dive without the presence of two IADA judges, and I found this both restrictive and expensive. What was wrong with *my* team?

Needless to say, I was in constant conflict with IADA. By the time I returned from the Caymans, where I felt stung by all the criticism and naysaying, I decided I'd had enough. It was time to stop seeking their certification. I was tired of being told that my records were unverifiable and therefore invalid. I was going to create an alternative organization that was less restrictive but equally viable.

My biggest problem was *making* it viable. I'm much better at conceptualizing than I am at executing, so I needed someone who could take this embryonic organization and put it on the map. The first person who popped to mind was Carlos Serra, my meticulously organized friend. He ran a spotless dive shop in the Keys, and ran dive classes that were organized with military precision, and he was exactly what I needed.

Audrey and I drove down to the Keys to see him.

"I want to make you president of the IAFD," I said.

"What the hell's the IAFD?" he asked.

"The International Association of Free Divers."

"Never heard of it," he said.

"That's part of the problem," I said. "I created it, and I'm trying to get it off the ground, and I need someone with your organizational skills to make it happen."

Carlos was tempted, but he was on the fence. He wasn't sure about giving up a lucrative gig to get into a sport that most Americans had never even heard of. Then again, he didn't own the dive shop. He had a part interest in the place, sure, but he often felt like a hired hand, and he had always wanted to go out and do something of his very own.

"Think about it, *socio,*" I said. "We could really make this happen. Not that long ago, nobody had heard of in-line skating or windsurfing, and look where they are today. Imagine if we got in on the ground floor. This sport is going to take off someday, man. *Soon.* It's challenging, it's a rush, and it doesn't cost an arm and a leg."

Carlos turned to look at Audrey. "What do you think?" he asked.

"I think Pipín is right," she said. "I'm new to this, but I'm already crazy about it. I think you guys can make this happen."

"*We,*" I said.

"Well, I hate to say this," Carlos said, sighing. "But I'm tempted."

Carlos was a dreamer, just like me. So we eventually became partners. Before long, he sold his interest in the dive shop and began to devise a business plan. The first order of business was to try to generate income, so we decided we would start by giving classes. We decided we would work with anyone, from absolute beginners to experienced competitors, and that we should try to partner up with world-class resorts, which might welcome the extra business. We also got to work on the ultimate free-diving manual, and on our website, where we could promote the organization, sell videos and manuals, and push classes. We decided we could even develop a signature line of spearfishing guns and fins, and Carlos began looking into that right away. Last but not least, we began to think about our next record attempt.

Carlos and I often clashed—we had wildly different styles—but we were good friends, and we knew we would do anything for each other. Plus, the organization was important to us both. Our futures depended on it.

Fortunately, just when we most needed it, Mares, the diving company, came through for us by offering to sponsor me again. The money was great, but the credibility was even better.

The next thing we knew we were on our way to Palma de Mallorca, Spain, to hold our very first free-diving clinic. That's where we met Pascal Bernabé, the schoolteacher, and his baby-faced diving assistant, Cédric Darolles, Audrey's "guardian angel." Thanks to them, the event was a big success, and by success I mean two things: one, all of the students went home happy; and two, we actually broke even.

The other nice thing that happened on this trip was that I went to Italy, to see my daughter. The reunion with Simona was formal, though not unfriendly, and seeing Francisca—all grown-up at seven—was pretty wonderful. I promised her that she would never again go more than six months without seeing me, and I am glad to say that I have kept my promise to this day. Unlike Luca, who saw me almost every day in Miami, Francisca didn't really know me, and I thought it was high time I fulfilled my obligations as a father.

Three months after our success in Europe, Audrey, Carlos, and I went to Hawaii, courtesy of our fledgling organization, to hold a spearfishing clinic and to try to create more converts to the sport. There was a large turnout, twenty people at $300 a head, and I think we were a big success there, too, but we got off to a pretty slow start. Carlos got things rolling by giving a lecture about free diving and spearfishing, including a little history, and followed it up by playing some videos (which were of course available for sale). By the time I arrived, the students were getting a little fidgety, and I launched into a rather lengthy lecture of my own. "People don't know how to breathe," I said, plunging right in. "They take it for granted. But it's actually a remarkable process which culminates with the exchange of oxygen and carbon dioxide in the alveoli of the lungs. We have three hundred million of these thin air sacs, and if we spread them out they would cover an area the size of a tennis court. Shallow chest-breathing is how most people breathe because they lead sedentary lifestyles. They're not really using their diaphragm and stomach muscles. There is a lot of wasted air in the bottom of their lungs. Deep, abdominal breathing is a healthier way to breathe because it makes use of the total volume of your lungs. Watch a baby breathe. His stomach goes in and out. He's doing it naturally. That's what you should strive for."

I could see I was losing them, and I could see Audrey, way in back, hiding shyly, as always, and making the universal sign to speed things up. In other words, it was time to get the hell off the stage.

We were a lot more successful in the water. We worked with the students for two days, and by the end of the event everyone seemed satisfied, especially the guy who speared that twenty-two-pound mahimahi.

When we got back to Miami, Audrey began to run the office. She had strong organizational skills of her own, which rivaled even Carlos's talents in this area. We found a nice space in a building in North Miami, and set up shop, and before long we looked like a genuine organization. Audrey was not a trained bookkeeper, but she went on instinct, and before long we had books, balanced accounts, and even a budget. We had an actual Rolodex, too, on and off the computer, a bank account with actual funds, and an appointment calendar.

"I feel like a businessman," I joked with her one morning. "Next thing you know you'll be asking me to wear a coat and tie."

Before long, we were so busy that we hired an assistant, Carolina Servigna. She and Audrey often went off to have lunch together, and they bonded, and I always wondered what they talked about behind my back. Guys get a little paranoid about these things, and I was no different.

"What are you two always laughing about?" I asked one afternoon.

"Oh, nothing. Nothing at all."

Right. Sure. Such sweet, innocent women.

I once heard Audrey refer to me as *pinche niño*. Roughly translated, this means "that damned pesky little boy." And one morning I walked in to find her doing an impersonation of me for Carolina. She was rubbing the top of her head and scratching the bridge of her nose, and then she turned and reached for the phone and screamed and cursed in Spanish. That was the point at which she saw me, and she quickly turned beet-red.

"That was very good," I said. "You had my accent and inflection down perfectly."

Audrey humanized the place. She cleaned out an old fish tank and stocked it with fish. She brought in French pastries and flowers. She sent birthday cards to our relatives and to crew members. She adopted a stray cat.

And she was like a curator. She decorated the walls with diving para- phernalia, most of which was connected to my diving records. How could I not love that? I am as egocentric as the next person; probably more so. She plastered posters and photographs of me across the walls. She even had one of my old wet suits on display, and she asked me to autograph it. I didn't turn her down.

She was also much more rooted in reality than I could ever hope to be. I always came up with these crazy schemes, and she always listened, no matter how preposterous they seemed. I was the mad explorer; she was my sane, pragmatic better half.

"I want to go to Antarctica for the coldest free dive ever."

"I want to organize a free dive into the wreck of the *Andrea Doria*."

"Do we know anyone in Hollywood? We could do celebrity dives in Malibu!"

I wanted to organize tandem dives and vacation packages to exotic locales, and I still hadn't given up on selling my series to Mexican TV. I had tried to reach Azcarraga, but I'd heard he was sick, and no one was returning my calls.

One day I came up with a completely insane idea: an underwater nightclub. Divers would wear special shoes and weighted belts, and we'd pump music through underwater loudspeakers.

"That would make conversation a little difficult, don't you think?" Audrey asked diplomatically.

"People don't go to nightclubs to make conversation!"

"Well, you're probably talking tens of millions of dollars."

"So what? We could work with existing hotels. They'd love it."

Audrey prepares for a dive.

"I think insurance might be a problem," Audrey said.

She had a way of weeding out the lousy ideas without destroying me. And even when she made me see that something I wanted to try couldn't possibly work, she always did it delicately, with a sensitivity that seemed to come to her naturally. And I didn't feel deflated by these reality checks; instead, Audrey made me feel as if she were simply making room for my next idea—which would almost certainly be the best idea I'd ever had.

By now I was convinced she'd lived *many* lives before this one. Maybe as a mermaid. Maybe as a bookkeeper. Maybe as a saint. Maybe as a therapist.

"Someday people will walk though airports carrying their free-diving sleds," I said. "Just like they carry golf clubs and skis."

"Someday," she said.

In yet another former life, Audrey was probably a mediator. Whenever I got into an argument, she was able to defuse it. And she always made sure I saved face.

One time I got into a screaming match with Carlos over a bill we'd received from the printer.

"What the hell did you do?" I said. "Have the damned dive manuals made up in fourteen-karat gold?"

"Do you want them to look professional or do you want them to look like a piece of shit?" he shot back.

At this point, Audrey intervened. She made me see that it was money well spent. The manual was destined to become the free diver's bible, she explained, and the quality would reflect well on our entire operation. But she also let Carlos know that this was something we should have discussed as a team *before* he committed to the expense.

What could we say? Carlos and I smiled sheepishly at each other and shook hands.

Early in 1998, I got a call from Emilio Azcarraga, the Mexcian media mogul—only it wasn't the same Emilio: it was his son. The elder

Azcarraga had passed away, but on more than one occasion he had talked about *Planet Ocean,* the idea I'd mentioned after that dive in Cabo.

"I'm interested," the younger Azcarraga told me. "How do we get into business together?"

I sent him a rough cut of the video we'd shot in Roatán, where Audrey and I had spent time with our dolphin friends, Copan and Maya, and he was instantly hooked. He offered us twelve episodes and a budget of $600,000. It was such a generous offer that there was really nothing to negotiate or discuss. We were in heaven. Not only was this the chance of a lifetime, but I was going to be producing the show with Audrey at my side.

For the next year, we worked on the series. One of our most memorable and ambitious shows involved the humpback whales in the treacherous Silver Bank Passage, between the Dominican Republic and the Turks and Caicos. The seas there are always incredibly rough, and during the voyage out, on the boat, we spent most of our time hanging over the side, throwing up.

For several days, we endured the torture, looking for these fifty-foot, fifty-ton giants. Each winter, some three thousand of them migrate down from Canada, but we couldn't find a single one. Then one morning, there they were, a regular army of humpbacks!

Within minutes, we were in the water, but the whales steered clear, wanting nothing to do with us. We kept trying, and returned the following day, but the best we could do was observe them from afar. They are truly amazing creatures. Their pectoral fins can be up to sixteen feet long. They communicate by beating their fins or tails against the surface and by emitting a wide range of sounds, and they've been known to "sing" for up to five hours at a stretch.

"I guess they don't do many encores," Audrey said.

We tried again the next day, and two of them approached, to investigate, but they didn't find us very interesting—they aren't predators: they eat plankton and krill—and off they went, with a single swoosh of their powerful tails.

The following day, still determined, we were back in the water. We had blisters on our ankles from the fins—the water was so rough we had to keep kicking—and I was on the verge of calling it quits. But just then a solitary whale appeared not twenty feet away. Audrey swam ahead of me, and I followed with the camera. The whale seemed curious. He allowed her to get so close that she could almost touch him. When she was forced to surface, to catch her breath, she was sure the whale would swim off. But he waited for her, and she dove in again and approached.

I got all of this on film. Neither of us was wearing scuba tanks, but I had attached tanks to the stabilizing wings of the camera housing, and I could take oxygen as needed and stay down. This time the whale let Audrey run her hands across its fins and back. I felt chills up and down my spine. This creature was ten times Audrey's size, and he could have swallowed her whole, but instead he was gentle and playful.

Later, on the boat, and still feeling very wired from the encounter, Audrey said it was unlike anything she had ever experienced. "I know this sounds crazy, but it was almost as if he were as curious about me as I was about him," she said.

"I don't think that sounds crazy at all," I said.

"I felt I was in the presence of a very wise creature."

Although we already had some pretty compelling footage, we decided to go back for one last day. Amazingly, we ran into a pair of humpbacks who weren't shy at all. They swam with us, completely unafraid, and at one point I got so close that our sides brushed together. A moment later, one of the whales broke into song, an eerie underwater hymn that sounded like the low-pitched chant of a Buddhist monk.

Audrey and I returned to the boat transformed.

"That was eerie," she said. "I almost felt as if they were calling to us."

Years later, I would remember those words.

When we returned to Miami, more connected and more in love than ever, Audrey told me that she wanted to meet my family.

"I want to spend time with your mother," she said, "and I want to see what you saw when you were growing up."

I was effectively banned from returning to my home country, so she went on her own and stayed in Havana with my mother. My mother was no longer working for the government, largely because my defection had made it untenable, but we had made peace with each other despite our ideological differences.

Audrey and Margarita, however, had no differences whatsoever. They bonded instantly. Audrey slept in my old bed. She visited my favorite haunts. She saw the cove where I had first fallen in love with the sea.

My mother took her strolling along the Malecón, past my old school, and into the heart of Old Havana, where she found a painting at the artist's market that she brought home as a gift for me. At night, my mother would make dinner—usually one of my old favorites: black beans, rice, fried plantains.

One day the two of them drove to Varadero and sat on the beach I knew so well.

"Pipín used to come here to watch members of the spearfishing team return from the sea with their haul," my mother said. "He was curious about anything to do with the water. Even as a little boy, he always wanted to go deeper and farther than anybody else."

"Well, that certainly hasn't changed," Audrey said.

"What is he looking for?" my mother asked her.

"I'm not sure," Audrey said. "Maybe the same thing we're all looking for. He's just trying to figure out what all of it means."

Audrey returned from Havana with a number of mementos from my youth. Diving trophies, medals, ribbons. My mother had hidden them in an old cigar box and stashed them at the bottom of Audrey's suitcase.

"Your mother misses you," Audrey said.

"She could come live with us tomorrow," I said.

"She'll never leave Cuba."

I picked up one of the medals. I'd won it twenty years earlier, for taking first place in the butterfly stroke, and looked at Audrey. "This reminds me," I said. "It's time for another record."

Audrey reached up and kissed me. She could see I didn't want to talk about home or my mother or my life in Cuba. Life is about forward movement. Like the sharks, we must keep swimming.

By the spring of 1998, I was talking to Seiko, the Japanese watchmaker, about an endorsement deal—better than the deal I'd had with Sector. They knew I was being sponsored by Mares, and that we were selling a full line of IAFD diving gear and spearfishing videos, and they had seen my brief appearances touting the sport on the Discovery Channel and in a *National Geographic Explorer* special. I guess they figured free diving was on the verge of breaking out. But it wasn't breaking out fast enough for me. In the minds of most Americans, the few who even thought about it, free diving was still a vague concept, and I was looking for new and flashier ways to exploit its potential. That's when I came up with the notion of a tandem No Limits dive. I thought that the sight of two people, perfectly synchronized, riding the sled as partners, could be a real attention grabber—not to mention a great deal of fun.

I had once thought of doing it with my idol, Maiorca, but he had long since retired. And when I approached Pelizzari, my old rival, he declined, dismissing the idea as another gimmick. I wasn't going to argue with him. Of course it was a gimmick, but that was only part of it. Tandem diving could be a whole new sport.

"Why don't we do it?" I asked Audrey. "It'll be the international debut of Tandem No Limits Diving."

"I'd love to," she said. "But I'm still an amateur."

"We can change that," I said. "You're a quick study."

We took the boat out and started practicing, and, initially, it was tougher than either of us had imagined. For one thing, before we even took the plunge, we had to coordinate our breathing to reach the optimal inhalation point at exactly same time. Then, on the way down, only one of us could control the rate of descent, and this made it hard for the other person—Audrey, in our case—to equalize her ears.

Then it got even more complicated. The first time we went beyond thirty meters, Audrey lost her grip on the lift bag on the way back. I didn't notice and kept ascending without her. But after several seconds I realized I was suddenly climbing much more rapidly, and I opened my eyes to find her gone. I stopped and went back for her, and we swam to the surface together.

One time we slid off the cable and flipped over, and I ended up upside down. Audrey helped me get my bearings and we went back up and tried again. By the end of the week, we had it right. We felt as synchronized as a pair of Olympic figure skaters.

"Let's go to Cabo and put on a real show," I said.

"What do you have in mind?"

"A triple feature," I said.

I thought we'd start with a tandem dive to 50 meters. Then Audrey would follow that by riding the sled alone to 115 meters, breaking the female No Limits record of 112 meters set the previous year by Deborah Andollo, a Cuban. And, finally, I would attempt another two-breath dive, this time to 155 meters.

When I got in touch with the people at Mexico's Departamento de Turismo, they came up with a brilliant idea. Apparently, there would be a show going on in Lisbon, Portugal, toward the end of May—Expo of the Oceans—and they said they might be able to broadcast our event live, on a jumbo screen. This would generate publicity for both Cabo and the sport.

We were thrilled. We went to Cabo in mid-May, to train. One afternoon, as Audrey was preparing a practice ride to a depth of 95 meters, I made a joke about riding along to make sure she was doing it right.

"Sure," she said glibly. "Hop on. There's plenty of room."

I thought she was joking—the deepest we had ever gone together was 50 meters—but I played along. "How far do you want to go?" I asked.

Audrey kissing me after I set a record in Cozumel.

"I'm going to ninety-five," she said.

She began ventilating, and I swam over, took the copilot's side—this was, after all, Audrey's dive—and began doing my own ventilations.

When Audrey was ready, she nodded and I pulled the cord. The sled splashed into the water and we went down like a bullet.

Thirty meters, 40, 50. Audrey was in control of the brakes, but she didn't reach for them until we hit 95 meters. We got off the sled, looked straight into each other's eyes, then she took my hand and kissed it. A split second later, she inflated the lift bag and we rocketed back to the surface.

Later that night, lying in bed in our hotel, I told Audrey that we could really milk the publicity by doing a tandem dive to 100 meters. "You had oxygen to spare down there," I said.

The next day, we decided to do a practice run, and we overshot our mark, going all the way to 116 meters. We could barely believe our depth gauges, but both of them couldn't be wrong. This was pretty amazing. It meant that Audrey had actually surpassed Andollo's record, and on a *tandem* dive.

We changed our plans again. We decided that Audrey and I would set a tandem record of 115 meters, which would also establish her as the new female champ. And I would still follow it up with a two-breath, 155-meter dive.

On the appointed day, we had to synchronize our countdown with the TV crew, who were going to broadcast the event live to Portugal. They told us that they expected a worldwide audience of more than 50 million people.

Everything sounded like it was on track, but we became quickly derailed. For starters, the spectator boats began to crowd us, and we could taste the exhaust fumes. It was very disconcerting, not to mention dangerous. The last thing you want before a dive is a mouthful of carbon monoxide. Next, the cameraman asked us to delay the countdown because the broadcast was behind schedule. Unfortunately, Audrey and I had already begun our ventilations, and there was no turning back. I don't think the man really understood the complexity of the sport.

"I can't do it," I said. "We're ready and the safety divers are about to go down."

He tried to negotiate with me, getting angry, but I wasn't about to risk either Audrey's health or my own. "Tell Portugal we're not waiting," I said.

The countdown began. I could hear the cameraman arguing with his producer, but at least the cameras were rolling.

I turned to look at Audrey. "Piece of cake," I said, and I pulled the release cord.

During the entire descent, our elbows were touching. I felt fused to Audrey in ways that went well beyond the physical. The ringing sound of the sled against the cable sounded like our very own version of a whale song. I slowed a little at the halfway point, giving Audrey a chance to equalize her ears, then we plummeted to the bottom. I quickly unhitched us and inflated the lift bag, and we sailed skyward, side by side. We broke through the surface in record time.

I could hear people hollering and cheering, but I was looking only at Audrey. She looked good. Her skin had good color and her eyes were clear. I kissed her.

"You did it!" I said.

"*We* did it."

A bouquet of red roses landed on the water next to us. I handed them to Audrey. I was overwhelmed with love for her. At that moment, I couldn't imagine what I'd done to deserve her.

"Are you crying, Pipín?"

"No, of course not," I protested. "I have no idea what you're talking about."

We did a few interviews—Audrey hated the cameras—then went off to shower and have dinner together. We went to bed sated and happy.

In the morning, with great fanfare, I did my two-breath dive. Something about it felt wrong, however—it was almost too easy—and when I surfaced, to the whirring cameras and the usual raucous cheers, I soon discovered what had happened: one of the members of the crew had forgotten to drop the line to the prescribed depth. I'd only gone to 115 meters, not to the record 155-meter mark I'd been after.

I was furious—the old, angry, combative Pipín was back in all his moody glory—and I took it out on the crew. Then I had to humiliate myself by explaining what had happened to the producers. "Somebody fucked up," I said. "I'm sorry. Give me a day of rest and I'll try again tomorrow."

The next day, the dive went beautifully. I'd set a record.

When it was all over, when all the fanfare had died down, I went back into the water to help retrieve the sled, and I returned to the boat and began babbling incoherently.

"My head really goddamn hurts," I told Audrey, and I promptly collapsed. The last thing I remember is somebody shouting out that I was bent, and hollering for an ambulance to meet us at the dock.

I woke up in a hyperbaric chamber and freaked out. "I don't have the bends!" I screamed. "Get me the hell out of here."

I could see Audrey and a couple of crew members peering through the porthole at one end of the chamber, and I began to pound away at the walls and tiny windows like a caged beast. The doctors, fearing I would hurt myself, let me out, and I flew back to Miami in pain and misery.

By the time we reached our house, on Treasure Island, I was groggy and disoriented and slurring my words. Audrey called Dr. Rick Prado, a spearfishing friend, and he met us at the hospital. He introduced us to Dr. Alex Forteza, one of the leading neurologists at Jackson Memorial Hospital. It was a good thing, too. I have very little recollection of the next few days, but Audrey later told me that I didn't seem to know where I was, who I was, or even who *she* was.

"Audrey who?"

"Audrey Audrey," she said, fighting tears. "The woman who loves you more than life itself."

Carolina, our assistant, was there every day, along with her husband, Chelique. I don't know how Audrey would have managed without their help and support.

I couldn't figure out how to use a phone, and the TV remote was truly beyond my comprehension. And at one point I even lost some of the motor function in my arms.

When I was slightly improved, Dr. Forteza told me that some nitrogen bubbles had probably become lodged in my brain. "You're going to be fine," he said. But I could see—even in my damaged condition—that he wasn't sure if I'd be fine at all. He wasn't talking to me as a doctor at that moment; he was addressing me as a friend.

Audrey stayed by my bed for an entire week. No one knew how extensive the damage was, or whether it would be permanent. Some of the effects seemed to be mirroring that of a stroke.

When Audrey finally got me home, I wasn't the same man. I had trouble with the simplest math. I couldn't remember names or dates. I didn't know my own phone number.

For the next two months, Audrey stood by me, a real soldier. I was a damaged version of the man she'd fallen in love with, but she loved me still. It was agonizing for her—I could see it in her eyes; could see the way she was always fighting tears—but she never broke down in front of me. She was always positive, sometimes almost desperately so. She convinced me that I would get better. She cooked for me and read to me and rented my favorite movies and took me for walks on the beach, and she would only leave me alone for two or three hours at a time, to go to the office and try to keep our business running.

For two months, we didn't talk about the diving. There was nothing to talk about, really. The water was my life. I would never quit, and she knew it. If it was my fate to die in the water, I would die in the water. In any event, it wasn't up to me. In the water, Olokun was in charge.

Day after day, week after week, Audrey waited on me hand and foot, my very own Mother Teresa. She never lost hope and she never let me lose hope.

I would have been lost without her.

↓

Chapter_ SEVEN:

BLACKOUT

Mexico, January 2000: I had to be lifted out of the water unconscious.

Eventually, I recovered fully, and I did what I'd been thinking of doing for the better part of a year: I proposed to Audrey. We were married on August 18, 1999, at sunset, at our home on Treasure Island, by a justice of the peace. The sky over Miami glowed lavender as we exchanged vows.

Audrey had picked out a pair of titanium wedding bands. We placed them on each other's fingers. She grinned, amused by all the formality, and I grinned right back at her. I didn't need a legal document to tell me that I was going to spend the rest of my life with this woman: I knew it in the deepest recesses of my heart. We had been together for three and a half years, and I loved her more than ever.

"You know, they say love fades over time, and I used to believe that," I told her. "But it only fades if you're with the wrong person."

"Who knew I was marrying such a romantic?" she said, kissing me.

"Don't tell anyone, okay? I wouldn't want it to get out. I have a reputation to protect."

The wedding party went well into the night, much to the chagrin of the neighbors, and when my wife and I finally crawled into bed, just as the sun was coming up, I gave her a little kiss on the forehead.

"I have something to say to you, Mrs. Ferreras."

"What?"

"I have never been happier in my life."

She kissed the top of my bald head. "I have never been happier in my life, either," she said.

We fell asleep in each other's arms.

Audrey and I always said that there were two types of people in the world: those who dipped a toe into life, and those who dove right in.

Audrey and I belonged to the latter group, literally and figuratively. And the deeper we dove, the deeper we came to know each other. For us, free diving was not only a living, but a way of life. Audrey used to describe it as an out-of-body experience. She forgot she was human, she said, forgot she had flesh and skin and bones. When she was diving, she felt like pure energy, a source of light.

I was less spiritual. Even after all the years and all the mishaps, free diving was still a hell of a thrill. I discovered something new about myself each time I went down, and I remained obsessed with going ever deeper. I felt like an explorer, venturing into the unknown. I didn't expect to be compared to Columbus or Neil Armstrong, but that didn't keep me from dreaming, or from trying.

Audrey and I were happiest in that silent, mystical underworld, bathed in blue. We had grown up at opposite ends of the world, thousands of miles away from each other, but early in our lives each of us had developed an unusual and abiding love for the sea. That love had only grown stronger, and in the years ahead it grew stronger still. Just before the plunge, engorged with oxygen, we felt somehow closer to our true selves. And when we returned to the surface, gasping for air, it was like being reborn.

I'd be less than honest if I didn't admit that there was an addictive element to the experience.

"Sometimes," Audrey said, "it's a real drag coming back up."

I knew exactly what she meant.

Audrey loved to draw, and she was a fine artist. Sometimes she would be in Audubon mode, and she'd sketch whales, turtles, seals, and sharks in their natural habitats. At other times, her work seemed closer to that of Salvador Dalí, the great Surrealist. In one self-portrait, she's a mermaid, naked from the waist up. In another, she's lying on her back in the water, her wild mass of luxuriant hair spread out like a giant fan. In still another, she's doing the tango with a dolphin. And in her most erotic self-portrait, she's lying under a reef shark, her legs wrapped around its body.

One day, while I was out on the dock, tinkering with the boat, Audrey took a seat on the bow and began to sketch. She drew a picture of a long-haired mermaid, pressed up against the belly of a hammerhead. The mermaid's arms seemed to be draped over the shark's pectoral fins, as if for support, and their two tails curled off in the same direction.

There was something astonishing about the drawing. The two bodies seemed to meld into one, and you couldn't help but be moved by the intensity of that closeness.

"It's beautiful," I said. "What does it mean?"

Instead of answering, she wrote two words at the bottom of the drawing—*Together Forever*— then she kissed the three middle fingers of her right hand and touched my forehead, as if anointing me.

"I feel like I've just been blessed," I said, smiling.

"I felt blessed the day I met you," she said.

A few weeks later, Audrey came home with a small tattoo of a shark on her left ankle, then followed it up by having my *signature* tattooed on the back of her neck, just below her hairline. I was overwhelmed. It was like a permanent valentine. For the next three or four nights, I rubbed cream into the bruised skin, trying to get it to heal faster. "You know, Audrey," I told her, massaging her neck. "In Cuba, only crooks and gangsters have tattoos."

"Well, there you go," she said. "I'm a gangster of love."

We led an idyllic existence. We had an outdoor gym set up on the dock, and every day we'd train to stay in shape. We'd lift weights, stretch, do crunches and breathing exercises (sometimes both of them combined), and every other day, come rain or shine, we'd hit the streets for a 10-kilometer run.

Audrey was almost religious about the workouts. She was five six and weighed only 125 pounds, but before long she was doing twice as many crunches as me. She could also make her heart rate climb to 210 beats per minute, which was a lot more impressive than my measly 185.

"Well," I said. "You're young."

"Please, God, not again," she'd say, laughing—and then she would mimic my voice perfectly: "Why, when I was your age, I could do a thousand crunches! I could run a four-and-a-half-minute mile! I could leap tall buildings in a single bound!"

"Ha ha. You're a regular comedian. Maybe you should audition for a spot on Letterman."

The truth is, age had nothing to do with it. When Audrey wanted something, she went for it. And when she went for it, she went for it one hundred and ten percent. After all, this was the woman whose mantra since early childhood had consisted of five simple words: "I can do it myself."

If the weather was good, we'd take the boat out for a few practice dives. And often, on our way back, we'd stop for a little spearfishing. We'd putter home and clean and cook the fish and eat it, often ending our evenings with a movie or a good book.

One sweltering afternoon, while the city baked, we took the boat out to Fowey Light and Audrey did a quick hundred-meter dive. She returned to the surface glowing. She made it seem so effortless that I told her she was ready to go to 125.

"I can't take the pressure on my ears," she said. "It's hard to equalize at that depth."

It *is* hard to equalize at that depth. The less air you can hold in your lungs, the less you have in store to help you equalize. I had a decided advantage over her in that department—my lungs were considerably roomier—but there was a way around it: wet equalization. This involved letting the water rush into your sinus cavities, which relieved the pressure as effectively as those blasts of air. Of course, it was quite unpleasant. It stung, and it made your head ache, and sometimes your nasal passages even bled a little. But those were small sacrifices for love of the sport.

"That was like putting a hose up my nose!" Audrey said after she tried it for the first time. "I felt like I was flooding my head with salt water."

She went back and tried again, and it was only marginally easier. "I can still think of one or two thousand things I'd rather do," she said.

One afternoon, we returned home to a message from a German film producer, Almut Saygin. I called back and found out she was hoping to make a short film about free diving, for Imax. She said she would also be talking to Umberto Pelizzari, since she intended to make it about the two of us, and about our divergent approaches to the sport. By this time, Pelizzari had pretty much abandoned No Limits. He was all about Constant Weight, relying solely on his own body to make the dive. I, on the other hand, was still obsessed with No Limits—and that's the right word, *obsessed*—with going deeper than any man had ever gone before.

"I'm definitely interested," I said.

"I'll be in touch," she said.

Weeks passed and we didn't hear back from her, and we went off to the Galápagos Islands, to film the next segment of our Mexican TV series, *Planet Ocean*.

When I first laid eyes on the place, I understood how Charles Darwin must have felt when he reached those craggy shores. We hiked over volcanic rocks, into craters, and across expanses of coffee-colored sand, and we saw a world teeming with forms of life that seemed almost unimaginable. Iguanas that swam. Dwarf penguins. Ancient, doe-eyed tortoises. And such a wide variety of seabirds that they were impossible to count.

On our very first dive, there was so much life and at such proximity that we didn't know where to look. There were seahorses, and spotted eagle rays, and a hawkfish that looked as if it had been designed by Versace.

The next day, we went diving among the corals off Wolf Island. "When I was little," Audrey said, "I used to tell my father all about coral reefs. I wish he was here to see this."

At one point, while we were filming, the light shifted, and I turned toward the surface to discover several dozen hammerheads gliding past, blotting out the sun. They kept coming and coming: not dozens, but *hundreds,* strange, prehistoric beasts with wide-set, all-seeing eyes.

"Were you frightened?" I asked Audrey when we surfaced.

"No," she said. "Nothing about the sea frightens me."

The next morning we explored the deep waters around Darwin Island, and found ourselves face-to-face with a whale shark. It was almost as large as a full-grown humpback, and it moved with effortless grace and majesty. We got so close we could feel the vacuumlike pull of plankton-rich water being sucked into its mouth.

There was a family of sea lions on shore, but every time I tried to approach they'd roar their hoarse roars and bare their big teeth. They seemed to like Audrey, however, and Carlos has footage of her on land, on all fours, practically rubbing noses with one of the giants.

Over the course of the next year, the series took us around the world. We went to Cocos Island, off Costa Rica, and swam with Tetsis, giant manta rays that look like huge spaceships. In Egypt, we explored the Red Sea. We fed sharks in the Bahamas. And back in Florida, along the Crystal River, we played with lumbering, amiable manatees.

We were busy all the time, and new things were happening every day. Then the phone rang one evening and I heard Almut Saygin on the other end.

"We got financing for the movie," she said brightly.

"The Imax movie?"

"Yes," she said. "We're calling it *Ocean Men: Extreme Dive.* It's the documentary version of *Big Blue.*"

"In other words," I said, "it's the real thing."

"Exactly," Almut said.

At that point I suggested that she talk to Bob Talbot, a hugely gifted underwater photographer, and I tracked him down myself and reached him in the Polynesian Islands, where he was doing what he loved best. I told him about Almut, and about the possibility of making an Imax movie, and within a week, he was back in Los Angeles. Almut flew in to meet him, they talked, and he immediately committed to the movie. He called me right after the meeting. "Thanks for setting this up, Pipín. I am thrilled to death."

I was thrilled, too. Unfortunately, as the project began to move forward, some of that old rivalry with Pelizzari reared its ugly head. First, we squabbled over money. Then we argued about the ground rules. It looked as if Pelizzari wanted to turn the experience into a No Limits contest, and I didn't understand that at all. He had moved away from the sport. Why, now, was he moving back?

But of course I knew the answer. There's a lot of ego in competitive sport, and neither of us lacked for ego. You don't make it in this or any sport—you don't make it in *life* –if you don't have ego. And we both had it in spades.

It goes without saying that each of us wanted to be the best, and it further goes without saying that each of us thought *he* was the best. Humility makes great saints but not great athletes.

Bob Talbot had his hands full. If he wanted to capture us trying to top each other, he knew he wasn't going to get us to do it in the same place. But he didn't really need that; that's not the way records were generally set, anyway. Pelizzari could dive in Sardinia, and I'd dive right here, at home, in Miami. But who would go first? Not me. If I went first, Pelizzari would simply try to beat my record—even by a lousy half-meter. I wasn't doing this to be second best. And Pelizzari felt exactly the same way.

Finally, we came up with a compromise. Pelizzari would set a Constant Weight record. He already felt that that category was more aesthetically pleasing and demanded more skill, so why not? I would stick to No Limits, and try to break the existing record of 150 meters, set previously by Loïc Leferme. That way, neither of us could lose. In fact, if we were competing at all, it was only philosophically.

I was pleased with the compromise. At that point, the only person I would be competing with, for the record, anyway, was Frenchman Loïc Leferme, who had set an AIDA-sanctioned No Limits record of 137 meters the previous June, off the coast of France.

Dominican Republic: Audrey doing yoga on the beach.

Talbot was also very pleased. He was less interested in the competitive aspects of the sport, and more interested in capturing its joy and beauty. He wanted the world to get to know a pair of men who seemed more comfortable in the water than they were on land; happier among sea creatures than among people. There was only one thing we wouldn't do: we wouldn't be filmed together, at *any* point in the film. These preparations for the shoot had been the last straw. By now, I couldn't stand Pelizzari, and he felt exactly the same way about me.

When the ground rules were finally in place, the producers sent over the contracts, and we all signed them, and Bob Talbot and his crew got to work.

The film was, by and large, a wonderful experience, marred only by two unpleasant episodes. When I look back on it, however, I have to admit that much of the fault was mine.

The first occurred when I flew to Nassau to film a few important scenes. I was with Audrey and my daughter, Francisca, who had come in from Italy to vacation with us and ended up staying for the duration of the shoot. As soon as we arrived at the hotel, I discovered that Pelizzari was still there, and I took Audrey and Francisca and turned around and went back to the airport, determined to hop on the next flight to Miami. Within the hour, however, Talbot and Almut arrived at the terminal and begged me to stay. They said Pelizzari was back in the hotel, packing, and was due on the next plane out.

I looked at Francisca, then at Audrey. "I'm being a little childish about this, huh?"

Audrey smiled that impish smile of hers. "I think I have to agree with you on this one, Pipín," she said.

We went back to town, Pelizzari left, and the following morning we began to film my segment. I was supposed to do an eighty-meter free dive, on the sled, which seemed fairly uncomplicated, but Talbot wasn't getting the angles he was after, and he kept asking me to do it again and again.

"Just one more," he said for the fifth time, at which point I blew up.

"Look," I snapped. "We're not making *Free Willy* here! I'm a man, not a whale that does clever tricks. Maybe you should stick to big fish."

I climbed out of the water and hopped aboard a skiff and went back to the hotel. Talbot was fuming, and Almut was near tears, and no one on the crew wanted to interfere. As I was packing my bags, Audrey and Francisca showed up.

"Why are you so angry, Daddy?" Francisca asked.

"Because these people are incompetent," I said.

"He just wants the movie to be as good as it can be," Audrey told Francisca. "And if he thinks it's not going well, it upsets him."

"Is it going to be good?" Francisca asked.

"It is if your daddy stays here," Audrey said, looking straight at me. "This is important for his career, and for the sport. And making movies is hard and complicated work. But you can't just quit. Not if you really care. If you really care, you see it through."

If not for Audrey, I wouldn't have stayed, and *Ocean Men* would never have been completed. She had worked her magic on me yet again. Every day, this woman at my side was making me a better man. Or trying, anyway.

I went out to make amends and apologized to both Talbot and Almut, in full view of the crew. The next day we went back to work and got the shot we wanted. And the following day, given our newfound camaraderie, Talbot suggested a shot of me diving to a nearby wreck. It was a dazzling sequence, and it was the sequence we used to open the film.

On the last day of shooting, we did a segment with a number of sharks, and it went beautifully. We were in a good mood, and the sharks were in a good mood. But Talbot needed one more sequence—a quick shot of a shark entering the frame—and a local diver was asked to try to lure one toward the camera. He did too good a job. The shark burst into the frame and took an angry nip at the diver, leaving a gash on his head that required two dozen stitches.

In the course of the film, Umberto went for his Constant Weight record and nailed it: a very impressive eighty-meter dive. Remember, this is Constant Weight. He went down and back under his own steam, with no sled, no weights, and no lift bag. It was quite the accomplishment, even I had to admit it.

But he followed this up by doing something I considered quite unsporting: he went into the water the next day, with a sled and a lift bag, and reached a new No Limits record of 150 meters. Worse still, the record was sanctioned by AIDA, the organization I'd been clashing with these many years.

I couldn't understand why Umberto had done it. I think he did it simply to piss me off. I hadn't shot my final dive for *Ocean Men,* and everyone knew that I had hoped to make it down to 150 meters. But that had been rendered meaningless now. I would have to go deeper if it was to count for anything.

Pelizzari had broken Loïc Leferme's record by thirteen meters, so I decided to break *his* record by fourteen meters. Childish? Perhaps. But, despite what you may have heard, competition doesn't always bring out the best in people.

We decided to shoot the final sequence in Mexico, where I had been building a steady following, and we were invited to shoot in Cozumel, a resort island off the Yucatán Peninsula. Cozumel is a very pretty spot, but its warm waters are fickle. Kim McCoy advised me to find another location. He said the strong currents could reach three to four knots, which could seriously destabilize the sled cable.

"This is not a good place for the dive," he said. "I'm asking you, for your health and for my peace of mind, let's look for another location."

But it was too late. The money was already in place, the crew was ready, and the resort was expecting us. "I can't change it," I said. "This train has left the station."

A few days later, while still in Miami, I got a very strange phone call from my lawyer. He asked me if I knew a guy called Tata Lanza.

"I sure do," I said. "What's up?"

Tata was an old friend from Cuba, the one I often went spearfishing with—the one who almost drowned off Varadero, when his leg got caught in that old fishing line. After all these years, he had finally surfaced, but not under the best of circumstances. Apparently, he'd just been arrested by national park officers in Mexico for poaching a species of conch that was on the country's endangered list. Tata needed someone to vouch for his good name, and in trying to track me down, he'd been directed to the office of my lawyer.

"I'll vouch for him any time," I told my lawyer. "Do whatever you can."

Fortunately, by the time my lawyer got back to the Mexican authorities, Tata had been released. It turned out that they'd made a mistake—they had misidentified the conch in question—and they sent Tata packing without so much as an apology.

When my lawyer called back with the good news, I asked whether Tata had left a number where I could reach him, but the only number he'd left was that of the police.

I hadn't seen Tata since 1983, when he married a Canadian woman and moved to Montreal, leaving me behind in Cuba, where I would remain for another decade. I hadn't thought about Tata in years, but suddenly I missed him.

"Isn't life strange?" I asked Audrey.

"Could you be more specific?"

"The way people come in and out of your life."

"You mean your old friend Tata?"

"Yes. We were inseparable as boys. Now I know nothing about him, except that he's somewhere in Mexico."

The phone rang at that very moment, and I answered it and found Almut on the other end. She was calling to make arrangements for the trip to Cozumel.

"I was just thinking about Mexico," I said.

A few weeks later, when Audrey and I arrived in Cozumel, the first thing we did was take a closer look at the water. McCoy had been right about the currents, but there was really nothing I could do at this point.

"Are you sure it's safe?" Audrey asked me.

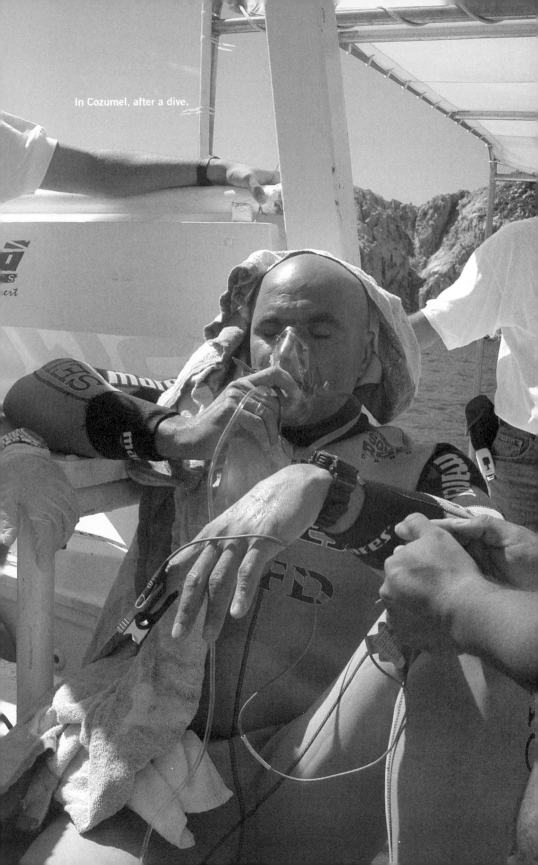

In Cozumel, after a dive.

"Yes," I said. "It might be a little tricky, but I can handle it."

When we returned to shore, I saw a bearded man who looked vaguely familiar. He was staring right at me, and suddenly he broke into a big grin. *"¿Cómo estás, socio?"*

I couldn't believe it. It was my old friend Tata Lanza. He had heard I was going to be in Cozumel and had come to thank me for my recent kindness. We gave each other a huge hug, and I introduced him to Audrey and Francisca, and that night, over dinner, we caught up on old times. Tata's marriage to the Canadian woman had fallen apart, and he'd been unhappy in Montreal, thousands of miles from the beloved ocean, so he had made his way across the United States and into Mexico. For a number of years he had worked as a spearfisherman in the Yucatán Peninsula, and he made ends meet, but he was open to new adventures.

"And being reunited with you," he said, "already feels like a new adventure."

"How would you like to be one of my safety divers?" I asked.

"Where do I sign up?" he replied.

From that day on, Tata became my chief support diver. We had spent countless hours in the waters off the coast of Cuba, and it seemed somehow fitting, and promising, that we'd been reunited. The next day, we went to work. Tata jumped into the water with me, to be there for my warm-up dives, and Tata was waiting for me when I came back—shadowing me during the critical last twenty meters of the ascent. I trusted Tata with my life. He was the brother I never had.

Later that evening, there was more joy: Audrey's parents had flown in from Mexico City, where they'd been living for the past year, happily relocated yet again. They had come to visit Audrey, and to watch me try to set a world record. Jean Pierre and Anne Marie were my new family, and we saw them often, and I couldn't have asked for better in-laws. When we returned to the hotel after dinner, Jean Pierre took me aside and told me something I'll never forget: "I have never seen Audrey happier."

When Audrey and I were back in the room, curiosity got the better of her. "What did my father tell you?" she asked. "Back there in the lobby?"

"He said he didn't understand what a good-looking Cuban stud like me saw in a scrawny little French broad like you."

She laughed and punched me in the shoulder. "What did he *really* say?"

"He said you looked happy."

"I am happy," Audrey said, and we got into bed and made love.

On Sunday, January 16, 2000, we went out to try to set a record of 164 meters. The weather was atrocious. The winds were gusting to thirty miles per hour, and the whitecaps made the water look like meringue. We decided that we were better off drifting, since an attempt to secure an anchor would have been hellishly difficult.

By the time we got into the water, the line was spinning off in all sorts of crazy directions, like a strand of derelict spaghetti. And just as we were about to start the countdown, the current seemed to intensify. It was as if Olokun himself were trying to send me a message. Several safety divers held on to the stern of the boat for support, only to find themselves getting towed out to sea. They struggled back, already exhausted, and we all tried to keep our heads above the choppy waves.

Kim shouted down at me from the boat, and the whipping wind made him almost impossible to hear. "Pipín! You don't have to do this! Let's postpone it!"

"That will screw up our whole schedule," I shouted back. I glanced at Talbot and the film crew, poised to roll. "Everybody's ready for the big dance," I hollered. "Let's just move to deeper water."

We went farther out into the channel. It was still windy and choppy, but I was committed, for better or for worse, and decided it was time to get ready.

When I tried to get onto the sled, the current ripped it right out of my arms, and Tata had to swim over to help me. I climbed back on, but I was very tired.

"You okay?" Tata asked.

"I'm fine. It's going to be great."

I started ventilating, but the sled was bucking like a bronco, and every other wave reached up and slapped me in the face.

I looked over at Audrey. "Begin the countdown," I said.

She looked at me pleadingly. She wanted me to call it off.

"Do it!" I said.

She glanced at her watch, wondering whether she might be able to talk me out of it this once. I could be a stubborn bastard, and I guess she saw the stubborn-bastard look on my face.

"Five minutes!" she hollered.

The safety divers disappeared into the churning water. I was having trouble staying on the bucking sled, and Tata swam over to try to hold it steady.

"*Mierda,* Pipín," he said. "This is bad."

I didn't answer. I looked up and saw Kim studying me, frowning. Everyone was being so damn negative, but I couldn't help myself. It was time to go. The cable was already drifting farther out of place, and the longer I waited the worse it would get. I took one last, gulping breath and nodded and Tata yanked the release just as a wave smashed into my face.

Boom! I was in the water, on my way. I could feel the swirling current, but it was relatively silent down here, and much calmer, and I rocketed toward the bottom at what felt like record speed.

I reached my goal—164 meters—and went to disconnect the sled. Damn! I couldn't get my fingers around the hardware. It took me 12 seconds to break free. I inflated the lift bag and shot upward, but the line was tilted at about 120 degrees, and it slowed me down horribly.

When I was about 10 feet from the surface, everything went dark. I had lost consciousness on that treacherous last leg of the journey. It's called "shallow water blackout," and it is a very insidious enemy. Just when you think you're home free, just when you're within sight of victory, your brain shuts down.

Physiologically speaking, it's fairly easy to understand. On the way down, the concentration of oxygen in the shrinking lungs increases as the pressure on the body increases. On the way up, as the pressure

decreases, the lungs re-expand, and the small amount of oxygen that remains inside them becomes diffuse. The lungs, desperate for air, begin to suction oxygen molecules from the blood. And the brain, relying on unoxygenated blood and literally running on empty, simply calls it quits.

There are more free-diving deaths from blackouts than there are from shark attacks or spearfishing accidents. I had blacked out in the past, probably a dozen times, but I always regained consciousness within seconds. This time I was not so lucky.

When I watched the video later, I noticed that my eyes were open but unseeing; that my face was bloated and blue; and that I was holding on to the sled in a virtual death grip. Two people on the boat jumped in to try to help, but Tata and Audrey were already in the water at my side and pushed them away.

"Wake up, Pipín!" Tata yelled, slapping my cheeks.

"Pipín!" Audrey screamed. "Can you hear me? Come back, Pipín!"

With some help, they hoisted my body onto the platform, and, as I saw from the video, everyone began to panic. This included Tata, who decided to give me mouth-to-mouth resuscitation—precisely the wrong thing to do. When one blacks out, you can't force them into consciousness. The organism is protecting itself, and it will fire up again as soon as the receptors decide it's *ready* to fire up. By forcing air into my lungs, or by pummeling my chest, as one of the other guys was doing, they could have done irreparable damage. Audrey was the only one who kept her wits about her.

"Get away from him!" she screamed, lashing out at Tata and the others with her small fists. "You'll only hurt him like that!"

I was out for about forty seconds, then my legs started twitching, and I moved my arms. I saw Audrey hovering over me, biting her nails furiously. Kim approached with an oxygen hose and I batted it away furiously.

I sat up and slipped back into the water, to get away from the pandemonium and to try to recompose myself.

"How bad was it?" I asked Kim, hanging on to the side of the platform.
"Pretty bad," he said.

"No," I said. "Couldn't have been more than ten seconds."

"It was closer to forty-five," he said.

"Bullshit," I snapped. "It wasn't that bad! I'm fine." Kim didn't say anything. I guess he didn't want to rile me further. "We've been through a lot worse, man," I said, "and we both know it."

By the time I was back on the boat, and marginally calmer, I got the bad news: the dive didn't count. I had made it to a depth of 164 meters, but I had not returned to the surface fully conscious, and that invalidated the attempt.

I went to bed in a lousy mood, and I spent the next day in a lousy mood. I was pissed at everyone, especially Olokun. I was even pissed at myself. I don't know what I was pissed about—just pissed that I'd lost consciousness, I guess. Pissed and feeling like a wimp.

Two days later, on January 18, my thirty-eighth birthday, I gave myself a little present: I tried again, in front of Talbot and his crew, and this time I nailed it. I didn't even hear the cheers as I came up. I was so happy that my ears were roaring.

The dive had taken 3 minutes and 21 seconds. I had purposely let out 165 meters of line to give myself a one-meter margin for error. Afterward, both my depth gauge and Pascal's gauge read 164 meters, but Kim's depth computer, the cylindrical gizmo I wore strapped to my back, had a reading of only 162. I argued with Kim, but I knew it was pointless. According to the rules of the game, you are obliged to accept the shallowest reading. And I didn't have any of AIDA's judges on the boat, so I needed a respected arbiter like Kim McCoy to give the dive credibility. I didn't need people questioning my world record.

And at the end of the day, I'd made it, right? It was a difficult week, and I had fallen a little short of my mark, but I had sent the free-diving community a message: *Don't mess with Pipín. Nobody beats Pipín.*

Ironically, despite all the proof—the gauges, the footage from the sled-mounted camera, the witnesses along the line and at the surface—

AIDA decided not to recognize the dive as an official record. I had not followed their rules or enlisted their judges. It was an *IAFD* record, and I ran the IAFD, so clearly—in their minds, anyway—there was a serious conflict of interest. They didn't think I was able to judge myself objectively. They didn't stop to think that *I* wasn't the judge. I had a team of professionals there, judging the dive, with the most sophisticated equipment around, and I had a slew of observers bearing witness from the sidelines. But it still wasn't enough for them.

"You don't need their blessing," Audrey said. "Everybody saw it, including a film crew. By the end of the year, people will be sitting in Imax theaters across the country, and they'll see what all of us saw here today."

The next day, everybody headed for the airport, including Audrey and I, along with her parents. Audrey had of course been telling them all along how much she loved the sport, but it seemed as if it hadn't sunk in until that last morning. Jean Pierre and Anne Marie were worried, as parents tend to be. They hadn't particularly enjoyed watching me lose consciousness, and they were even less thrilled when Audrey let slip that she was hoping to make a 125-meter dive.

Jean Pierre took me aside at the terminal, but this time it wasn't to talk about his daughter's happiness. It was her future he wanted to discuss. "Pipín," he said in a somber voice. "I don't think Audrey should be contemplating such a big dive. I saw what happened out there, and I didn't like it. You could have died."

"The sport is really not that dangerous," I said. "What you saw out there was the result of a combination of unfortunate factors."

Audrey joined us, and Jean Pierre turned toward her and took her face in both his hands. "Audrey, honey, are you really so committed to this . . . this sport?"

"Yes," she said.

"I'm sorry to be like this, but you're my only daughter and I'm worried and I want you to know I'm worried."

"You have nothing to worry about," she said. "You know me. I would never do anything I couldn't handle. I know my limitations."

It was not the answer Jean Pierre had been hoping for. If he had his way, she would have sworn there and then never to get on one of those damn sleds again. But Audrey had grown to love the sport as much as I did.

"I still don't get it," Jean Pierre said, shaking his head. "What's the point?"

"I'm not sure," Audrey said. "It's about going to the limit. It's about seeing how far you can go."

Jean Pierre remained at a loss. "I have something to tell you, and I want you to understand that I'm not doing it to punish you," he said. "I don't think I can handle watching you do this, so please don't invite me to any of your future dives."

Anne Marie had her own way of looking at it. "I'm not sure I approve, either, but I'm glad to see you're doing something you love. Few people ever get that opportunity."

We walked them to their gate just as the Mexico City flight began to board, then hugged them and said good-bye and hurried down the concourse to catch our flight to Miami.

"You okay?" I asked Audrey.

"Sure. Great."

"I thought your father was a little hard on you."

"He wasn't being hard on me. He's just being a dad. I'm his only child. He can't handle the thought of something happening to me."

I stopped Audrey and spun her round to face me and took her in my arms. "Well, you're my only wife," I said. "And I love you. And I can't stand the thought of something happening to you, either."

I kissed her, and to this day I remember that moment with a vividness I can't explain. Audrey and I, standing in the middle of the busy terminal, our lips locked together, very much in love.

It is an image that will stay with me forever.

Audrey doing breathing exercises before a dive in Spain.

*   *   *

In May, Audrey and I went back to Palma to try to set a new female record. Since our return from Cozumel, Audrey and I had been practicing near home, and we both knew she was ready. There were only four males, me among them, who had gone beyond the 125-meter mark, but Audrey would be the first female. The feat, if successful, would establish her as the sport's leading female diver.

We also hoped to do a tandem dive, and, when both those records were out of the way, I intended to try to break my own No Limits record. As far as I was concerned, it was still a record—AIDA be damned.

Those first few days in the water were all about Audrey, and she was in fine form. She was her usual fearless, confident self, and she was chomping at the bit to get going.

By the third day, I began to prepare for my own dive, and for some strange reason I felt a little off balance. I think it was largely psychological. The experience in Cozumel had been unpleasant, to say the least, and deep down inside I think I dreaded an instant replay. I hated the feeling. All my life, I had been a problem-solver. Put me in a maze with ten other people and I'll be the first one to find my way out. But this was different. I didn't feel like myself. The last dive had planted a seed of self-doubt, and I felt like a diminished version of the real me.

Partly as a result of these gnawing feelings, I was intentionally vague about the mark I planned to set. I figured I'd see how the practice dives went before I committed to a number. I hadn't been training as assiduously as Audrey, not since Cozumel, anyway, and I felt a little rusty.

Right from that very first practice dive, I was uncharacteristically uneasy. The sled was supposed to be my throne, but it felt like a torture rack. I blamed it on the unfamiliar environment, and told myself to ignore it and press on.

That first day, I set the line for eighty meters, a walk in the park. And when I pulled the cord and began to drop, I felt perfectly fine. But somehow, inexplicably, I reached the halfway mark and found myself thinking that I wasn't going to make it. I didn't even hit the brakes; I pushed myself off the plummeting sled and swam to the surface.

"Ear problem," I told the startled safety divers at the surface. "Probably the jet lag."

I tried again the next day, and the exact same thing happened at the exact same point. As I swam back to the surface, I could feel my heart pounding in my chest. *What the hell is wrong with me?* I was mad at myself and, worse, I was embarrassed.

"Sorry, guys," I said. "It's not going to happen. Not today, anyway."

Something was missing. That feeling of invincibility was gone. I used to be able to summon it at the snap of my fingers, but now I felt as if I'd lost it altogether.

When I got back to the beach, I decided to take a walk.

"You want me to come with you?" Audrey asked.

"No, thanks," I said. "I need a little time alone."

I walked about a half-mile, to a quiet grove of palm trees, and sat down in the shade to try to meditate. It didn't work. I felt as if I'd had too many cups of coffee, though it had been hours since I'd had anything to eat or drink. I tried to focus on the lapping waves and the gentle shushing of the palm trees, but nothing worked. My muscles were taut. I felt uncomfortable in my own skin. I wasn't myself at all.

I wondered if Olokun was trying to send me a message.

I went back into the water that afternoon, to try again. This time, it was even worse. I made it down to eighty meters without a hitch, listening to the singing of the cable, and I got the lift bag inflated in no time flat. But it turned out that the current had swept the line under a boat, and I shot toward the surface like a torpedo, oblivious. By the time I saw the hulking shadow above me, it was too late. Tata tried to soften the blow by putting himself between the fast-rising lift bag and the boat, but I hit the bag's ring and managed to cut a three-inch gash in my scalp.

Tata helped me to the boat, though he'd taken a bit of a banging himself.

"I don't know what's wrong with me," I told Audrey that evening. "But I know I'm not ready."

"Do you have any idea what it is?" she asked. I could see the concern in her eyes, but I could also see she didn't want to push me.

"I don't have a clue," I said. And I didn't. I really truly wanted to know what was going on inside me, but I haven't always been the most introspective guy in the world. Maybe that kind of self-awareness took practice, and I was fated to remain forever in the dark.

"I'm done diving here," I said. "But I want you to do your one twenty-five."

"You sure?"

"Yes," I said, and I could see what she was thinking. "I know what the sponsors are expecting from me, but I can't deliver." Then I started getting angry. "It's too goddamn much to supervise. Three different events. And I have to do everything myself if I want it done right. I can't concentrate on my record right now, okay!"

"Honey, calm down."

"I am calm!"

She gave me a moment to pull myself together. I wasn't anywhere near calm. I was shouting at her. I was shouting at the woman I loved, and for no reason either of us could fathom.

"I'm sorry," I said.

"Don't apologize," she said. "I just need to know what's wrong."

"I don't know. I wish I knew. Why don't we just drop it? We're here, you're going to set a record, and everything's going to be great. I don't need to be the center of attention all the time."

When I got in touch with the sponsors the following morning, they weren't exactly thrilled. But they didn't have much choice. I told them to make the most of it. I said Audrey would not disappoint.

On May 13, 2000, with 150 people watching, Audrey released the sled and rode it down like a bullet. She completed the 125-meter run in record time, but when she went to decouple the lift bag it wouldn't separate from the sled. When I reviewed the video later, I noticed that she had kept her wits about her. It's not easy to do. When an elevator gets stuck, three out of four people begin to feel that first hint of panic within seconds. Now imagine if you're stuck in an elevator that's 125 meters below the sea, and that you have only enough air in your lungs to make it to the surface, if you start moving *now.* Well, that was the situation Audrey was in. And she was unflappable. Instead of worrying about the clock, she fiddled with the pin. By this time, Pascal had entered the frame, to try to help, and just then the pin came loose. Audrey inflated the bag and shot to the surface, clocking in at an impressive two minutes and three seconds, despite the seventeen seconds she'd lost doing battle with the pin.

"That was a little scary," she told me later. "But it was okay. I never lost my cool. And I had Pascal right there, so I wasn't worried."

That evening, after we reviewed the video, I told Audrey I was very impressed at the way she had handled herself. Pascal was impressed, too. He high-fived her and gave her a big hug.

"That was really something, Audrey," he said. "No fear, no worries."

"That's me, baby," Audrey said, laughing.

They were being cocky, sure, but justifiably so.

That night, in honor of Audrey's record, we went to a reception hosted by a couple of local dignitaries. There was a buffet and a band, and it was all first-rate. Audrey and the rest of the crew were in a festive mood, and with good reason. They'd come to Spain to show the world what she could do, and they'd accomplished their mission.

I was part of it, too, of course. I had trained Audrey and I had supervised the operation. But I wasn't feeling particularly festive. In fact, I didn't even want to be there. I wasn't sure what was wrong, but I blamed my mood on that strange, dark cloud that had been following me around for several days. There was more to it than that, however.

I watched the way everyone was hovering around Audrey. I had told her that I didn't need to be the center of attention, and I thought I had

Getting ready in Cozumel.

meant it, but now I wasn't so sure. She was the burning candle in the center of the room, and all the guests were moths.

I tried to tell myself it didn't bother me, but I'm human, and the truth is that it *did* bother me. Don't get me wrong: I was happy for Audrey. But I felt lousy about myself. And standing there, watching her across the room, in the limelight, actually enjoying the attention for once—well, it did something to me. It made me feel very small.

It's odd. Audrey was an unusually good and loving person, and everyone she came into contact with felt it right away. As I've said, she seemed somehow more evolved than the rest of us mere mortals. People from all walks of life were drawn to her.

Even the guys on the crew, a real disparate bunch, were absolutely crazy about Audrey. She was one of them. She would talk with the guys, eat lunch with them, ask them about their lives with genuine interest. And she always stayed on the boat until all the safety divers had finished decompressing, which could take four or five hours. Audrey had been known to dive into the water to take a snack to a diver who'd been below for a while, decompressing. And sometimes she'd just go down to visit, to keep them company for a minute, or to write a little message on the slate: "Steak and ice cream for dinner!"

I was less patient and less giving. I could never stand the interminable wait after my dives, so I'd hop on the skiff and head back to the beach. Looking at Audrey there, still glowing in the center of the room, I thought about all of this and realized there were a lot of things about myself that needed work. I wasn't patient. I wasn't particularly giving. I seldom took the time to make the crew feel appreciated.

And thinking about this only made me feel worse.

I watched the reporters surround her, their cameras whirring and clicking, their notepads at the ready. I had an ugly thought. I wondered if Audrey was suddenly going to be seduced by the attention. I wondered if it would change her.

"Señorita Mestre," one reporter asked. "Tell us what it feels like to go so deep. Isn't it frightening in the darkness?"

Audrey turned and caught my eye. She signaled to me and I approached, albeit reluctantly. "My married name is actually *Ferreras*," she told the reporter. "And this is my husband, Pipín, the world record holder, as I'm sure you all know."

I smiled my gap-toothed smile and rubbed my bald head, but nobody was even looking at me. They had already turned their attention back to Audrey.

"How can someone as slim as you withstand the pressure at that depth?"

"What is it about the sport you love so much?"

"When can we expect you to try for another record?"

Audrey dutifully answered all their questions. *It's all about willpower. I love challenging myself. Within the next year, perhaps.*

When the mayor came over to shake her hand, I went to the bar and got myself a beer. Then I stepped out onto the balcony and looked at the dark, churning sea. "Pipín, you dumb bastard," I said to myself. "What is wrong with you? You should be happy for her, and for yourself. This is the woman you love. Get it together."

I had some demons in me, to be sure, but I realized that they had nothing to do with Audrey or her accomplishments. They were your basic run-of-the-mill demons: I was getting older. I had lost my nerve, if only briefly. I wasn't feeling good about myself. I was wondering, worriedly, if I had peaked.

Jesus! All this negativity. It had to stop. It was a sign of weakness, and I'd never been weak in my life. I would handle this. I'd get back in the groove.

When we returned to Miami, Audrey's fame took off. She signed a deal with Seiko, the watchmaker, and got a contract of her own with Mares. Everyone seemed to think she was a rising star, and I wasn't going to argue with them.

If Audrey could do 125 meters, she could do another five or ten or even twenty. She was twenty-six years old and unscathed by the sport.

She had a huge career ahead of her, and I was her most ardent fan. Every day, I'd burst into the office with a new idea.

"Let's set her next record in Japan/Australia/Brazil!"

"Let's get an endorsement deal with Clinique or L'Oréal! She's more beautiful than any of those girls."

"Let's talk to Imax about another movie: *Ocean Women.*"

Audrey and I would take Carlos and Carolina to lunch, and I'd go on and on about the future, one idea crazier than the next. "It's spring break in Fort Lauderdale! We'll have an amateur free-diving contest within a hundred yards of the beach. We'll ferry the students back and forth. The winner gets a sled from Mares."

"Sure," Carlos said. "And then we'll have a wet T-shirt contest!"

"I wonder if we could do it on live television, like that stunt we pulled with the feed to Lisbon. But locally. A *Wide World of Sports*–type thing. I know Audrey can do one forty."

One day we got into a huge argument about this. Audrey felt I was pushing her. "I don't give a damn about records!" she screamed. "You're all about records. I just like to dive."

"Oh! You don't give a damn about records, huh? You seemed to be enjoying the attention in Spain! I thought that was pretty cute when the mayor came over and kissed you."

"So that's what this is about? You're jealous!"

"I'm not jealous!"

The fight escalated until Audrey packed a bag, called a cab, and went to the airport. I didn't rush to stop her. I was seething. But as the minutes turned into hours, I began to worry. I called the airlines to try to find out if she'd gone off to Mexico, to be with her parents, but of course they wouldn't give me the names of the passengers.

Four hours later, she was back.

"What the hell are we fighting about anyway?" she said, dropping the suitcase at her feet, by the front door.

"I don't know," I said. I went over and gave her a big hug. "I love you, Audrey. I'm sorry. I can't make it without you."

Audrey preparing for a dive. That's Bob Talbot in the background.

We never fought like that again. Oh, we fought—don't get me wrong. We fought about the same things all couples fight about. Money. Respect. Love or lack thereof. But we always made up quickly.

"You know the weirdest thing about our arguments?" I said.

"What?"

"When we're in the middle of them, I can't for the life of me figure out what we're arguing about."

"I know," she said. "Isn't it ridiculous?"

"Let's try not to argue," I said.

"Deal," she said.

In the morning, Audrey was up early, making breakfast for my son, Luca. It was a routine we had. She would get up, make a quesadilla with white cheese, one of the few things on Luca's list of acceptable foods, then I'd drive over to Yamile's house, pick him up, and take him to school. He would eat the quesadilla en route, though sometimes, if he was still hungry, we'd stop at McDonald's for an Egg McMuffin and fries. I know it wasn't the best breakfast for a kid, but he was my kid, and he'd look at me with that little face of his and I couldn't resist. Luca was almost six years old and had just started kindergarten. When I dropped him at school, he marched inside like a little soldier, his lunch pail swinging at his side. It was enough to make me feel like crying.

I didn't have much of a relationship with his mother, unfortunately. I don't know whether Yamile was mad at me for getting on with my life, or mad at herself for having given up on me too soon. She should have had more confidence in me. I had never lacked for confidence, until recently, anyway. I imagine Yamile wasn't exactly thrilled by the fact that Luca was in love with Audrey, and I know he went home at the end of the weekend with all sorts of stories about his wonderful, beautiful step-mother.

As for Francisca, she came to visit often. I didn't have any problems with Simona. Part of it was the distance, of course—she was in Italy, thousands of miles away—but part of it was that she was still the strong, independent woman she had always been, and she wanted nothing from me. On the contrary, I had surpassed expectations. I think she was very pleased that I had begun trying to fulfill my obligations as a dad, and, to be honest, I felt pretty good about it myself.

Before long, Audrey and I began to plan our next event. We wanted to do something different this time, and came up with the International Festival of Tandem Diving. We got funding in Aruba, the Dutch island in the Caribbean, just off the coast of Venezuela, and I invited a couple of divers who were affiliated with AIDA, my least favorite organization in the world. That had been Audrey's idea. She said all the arguing only made us look like children, and she felt it was high time we got over it. I went so far as to invite AIDA to come to Aruba to sanction the dives and validate the records, if any.

Within days, Loïc Leferme of France agreed to dive with me. He's the one who had that 137-meter, AIDA-sanctioned record under his belt. And Mandy-Rae Cruickshank, a world-class, Canadian-born free diver, agreed to partner up with Audrey.

The women went first and wowed the crowd with a flawless, 110-meter dive. But when Loïc and I took the plunge, things didn't go quite so smoothly.

We were trying for 118 meters, and the descent went smoothly. But the pin jammed and we lost twenty seconds on the bottom. We finally got the lift bag inflated and were rocketing back, when suddenly the sled started twirling around the line. Loïc kept his cool, but I made the mistake of fighting the damn thing, and I used up a lot of oxygen in the struggle. Just as the surface came into view, I blacked out.

Apparently, I was out for a full minute. Audrey had begun to give me CPR. In the photos I saw later, my fat, purple face looked ghoulish, and Audrey and Tata were yelling into my ears.

"Pipín, talk to us! Pipín, come back!"

When I woke up, I had lost the feeling in my legs, and I was wildly combative. "Leave me alone," I shouted. "I'm fine. Get away from me!"

Eventually, my legs returned to normal, but my mood stayed black, and it remained black all the way home to Miami. I was convinced that the whole fiasco had been an AIDA conspiracy. I told Audrey that they had deliberately sabotaged the line. I said that the bastards were out to kill me, plain and simple.

Audrey just nodded and tried to be supportive. She could see what I failed to see: that what I was really angry about was my own failure; that I was simply doing battle with myself.

As soon as we returned from Aruba, Audrey made me go to see my old friend Dr. Forteza. A CAT scan of my brain showed several dangerous lesions. They were white on the screen but they were, in effect, my own personal black holes.

"You have a body made for free diving," Dr. Forteza told me. "And it has served you very well. But you've pushed it too hard for too long. All the dives, the quick ascents, the decompression hits, the oxygen deprivation—it adds up. You've probably gutted out the bends a few times without even knowing it."

"Oh, I knew it," I said. "Believe me."

"You're a lucky guy, Pipín. You've never had a major hemorrhage or an embolism. But you've taken a beating. If you don't want to end up in a wheelchair, or worse, you've got to give your body a rest. You've got to give the damaged nerve cells a chance to rejuvenate."

I went home in a dark mood, but Audrey helped me through it. She thought I should follow the doctor's advice and take a break. As she pointed out, no one was even preparing to challenge my record. And even Umberto Pelizzari had recently announced that he was officially retiring from No Limits competition, which he now found too dangerous.

"By the time someone comes along and tries to beat your record, you'll be well rested," Audrey said. "And if you feel like getting back into the water, you'll be ready."

It was good advice, and I took it. In fact, in some ways, it was a relief. I needed a break. I'd been doing this my whole life. And I loved it, yes. But I was exhausted.

I wasn't done with free diving, though. Not by a long shot. I decided to funnel my energies into Audrey's career. I wanted only the best for her, and I began to live, and *dive,* through my amazing wife.

Almost immediately it occurred to me that Audrey didn't have any issues with AIDA, and that it made sense to try to put their stamp of legitimacy on her next attempt. There was no reason she should be penalized for my ongoing feud with the organization.

On May 18, 2001, during Fort Lauderdale's Ocean Fest diving fair, we did a mixed tandem dive to 100 meters. It was 15 meters shy of the dive we'd done in Cabo, but that one had never been recognized by AIDA. This time, the AIDA judges were in attendance, and they confirmed the results.

The next day, Audrey did a solo dive to 130 meters. She was down and back in one minute, fifty-six seconds. The time, and the depth, were again sanctioned by AIDA, as well by our own organization, IAFD. It was the first No Limits world record set in the United States and the first to be recognized by both organizations.

Unfortunately, Audrey didn't hold the record for long. In September, Mandy-Rae Cruickshank rode the sled to 136 meters, in Grand Cayman. And later that fall, to add to the family funk, Loïc Leferme made a 154-meter dive in Saint-Jean-Cap-Ferrat, France. It was 8 meters shy of my own record, but mine had never been confirmed by AIDA.

In the summer of 2002, Tanya Streeter dropped the biggest bomb— and, as far as we were concerned, it was a bomb in more ways than one. She went to the Turks and Caicos and reached the 160-meter mark. AIDA declared it the new overall world record, but many aficionados of the sport, me among them, had a hand time believing that Streeter had held her breath for three minutes and twenty-six seconds. Audrey had done 130 meters in a scant one minute, fifty-six seconds. If Audrey could add another minute and twenty-six seconds to her breath-hold time, she could easily do 200 meters, and that didn't seem within the realm of possibility.

Streeter and I didn't get along. We had only met a few times, but she had issues with both my personality and my methods. She said I was a walking case of bravado. She'd seen me in action and accused me of being verbally abusive, though for the life of me I had no idea what she was talking about.

She was openly critical of my procedures, saying I should use more safety divers and equip them with backup lift bags. She was an attractive, articulate blonde, educated in England, but she bugged the hell out of me. Once AIDA had certified the dive, it almost made things easier for me: I didn't think much of the organization, so, as far as I was concerned, Streeter ceased to exist.

By this time, I had concluded that Audrey was ready for a 150-meter dive, and I was contemplating a last hurrah of my own: a stupendous, unheard-of 180-meter plunge. We were thinking of taking a stab at it in December 2002, but we decided to go sooner. The plan was to have Audrey break Streeter's record in October, so that she could show up at the annual DEMA convention as the undisputed queen of free diving. DEMA, the Diving Equipment and Marketing Association, is as big as it gets in our business, and the victory—a victory within the realm of possibility—would be a huge public relations coup for IAFD.

I know, I know. It sounded childish, and it probably was. But isn't that the nature of competition? Think about it: *I'm better than you. I'm stronger. I'm faster. I'm tougher.* It all boils down to a simple phrase: *"¿Quién es más macho?"*

At first, I thought about preparing Audrey for a 161-meter dive, which would have put her ahead of Streeter, and only a single meter behind my own record, set in Cozumel two and a half years earlier. But then I figured that Audrey should try to match my record. AIDA may have ignored it, but just about everyone else still spoke of it as the deepest free dive in recorded history.

I had set it during the filming of *Ocean Men*. Maybe she could do hers for *Ocean Women*? Of course, there were no plans for another Imax film at the time, but dreams die hard.

"You like the idea?" I asked Audrey. "We'll be the first couple of the sport. Audrey and Pipín. Husband and wife. Champions."

"I don't know," Audrey said, scrunching up her nose. "I don't feel like competing against my own husband. I'm not as obsessed with all of this as you are. I don't have to be number one."

"What about Streeter?"

"You're right about Streeter," she said pensively. "I wouldn't mind beating Streeter. Maybe I'll go for one sixty-one."

It was a big leap, admittedly, an increase of thirty-one meters in a sport where one generally moves along in very small increments, but Audrey didn't seem at all fazed by the idea. She had never had a physical problem during any of her dives, and she knew we could always scale back if at some point during the practice dives she felt any discomfort whatsoever. On the other hand, I got the distinct impression that she was holding back.

"Audrey," I said. "Let me tell you something. I want you to beat my record. It would be a dream come true."

"Are you serious?"

"Absolutely. This is our sport. We own No Limits. It would be *our* record."

When I look back on it, I realize that I was pushing her—pushing her as hard as I tended to push myself. And because she trusted me, my faith in her fueled her own self-confidence. If I thought she could do it, who was she to argue? In retrospect, as is often the case, I now see it much more clearly: it was blind ambition on my part, and blind devotion on hers.

"I know you can do this," I said. And I believed it, too. Watching Audrey evolve into a world-class free diver had been an eye-opening experience. She had a mind that wouldn't quit; a mind that truly accepted no limits. I knew I could learn a great deal from her, especially at that point in my career.

She had been my student once. Now she was my teacher.

↓

Chapter_ EIGHT:

UNFATHOMABLE

Getting used to the chilly water before a dive.

In late September 2002, we went to the Dominican Republic to watch Audrey set a world record. We had contacted several members of our loyal crew, and every last one of them had answered the call. They had to leave their regular jobs, pack their bags, and fly in from all corners of the globe to join us on yet another unpredictable expedition, but they were more than willing.

In an earlier era, these were the type of guys who would have sailed with Magellan or Columbus. To them, the sea was irresistible, and to plumb its depths was an adventure none of them could pass up.

The only downside was dealing with me. Audrey had done a great deal to smooth out my rough edges, but there was a limit to her power. A man can be wonderfully refined by the woman at his side, but he can't become a new man entirely, and I was still me, still unpredicatable, still bouncing between the two extremes of my Jekyll-and-Hyde personality.

Audrey was my polar opposite: a steadfast angel. People who found it tough to put up with me did so mostly because of her, even when the dives had been exclusively about me. This dive, however, was exclusively about Audrey, and everyone came. Pascal Bernabé, one of the most experienced safety divers on the planet. Kim McCoy, oceanographer extraordinaire. Party boy Wiky Orjales, the tough-as-nails scuba instructor I'd known in Cuba. My other formerly long-lost childhood friend, Tata. Burly Matt Briseno, who'd flown in from Hawaii. And of course Carlos Serra, the Venezuelan logistician, the band leader, the guy who had to take all these disparate personalities—mine, especially—and somehow make them work together.

On this particular dive, Carlos had his hands full, mostly because I wasn't diving and kept trying to make myself useful on the surface, generally without success.

But my restlessness was the least of it. We were all concerned about the magnitude of the attempt. Some of the guys were worried that Audrey was going too far, too fast, and it made for a certain amount of tension. We tried to break the tension over dinner at the resort, joking and laughing and horsing around, but it followed us everywhere we went.

Much of the discussion in those first days was about the safety divers. On a 162-meter dive, with Pascal at the bottom, we probably should have posted another diver at about 125 meters. That would have been Cédric's position, but he was dead, and the thought of replacing him weighed on us all. Carlos actually suggested that we use a Fort Lauderdale diver who had been with us when Audrey set her 130-meter record, but somehow we decided against it. I think we felt we'd be fine with Pascal at 162 meters and Wiky at 90. It was a big gap, yes, and Carlos continued to express concern, but trouble usually happens at the very bottom, whether technical or psychological, or at the very top, in blackout territory, so we let it ride. The fact is, these record No Limits dives often put the safety divers themselves at considerable risk, as we knew only too well, and we didn't want to gamble with the life of a diver who might have trouble at that depth.

We did, however, find an experienced local diver to help us out at the 60-meter mark. But for the critical final phase, up near the top, I was going to rely on Matt Briseno, Tata, and myself.

I went over the plans with Audrey and asked her if she approved. "I couldn't be happier," she said.

Neither could I: we both had complete faith in the team.

Audrey was as focused as I'd ever seen her, and in the best shape of her life. The conditions were perfect; the ocean was as calm as a pond. And the only time we had any trouble was on her very first practice dive.

That took place on October 1. We had set the cable for 115 meters. Pascal was at the bottom. I was on scuba at 80 meters, photographing the dive. I was fiddling with the camera when I felt something hit me in the back. It was the sled, and Audrey was on it. Needless to say, we were both pretty startled. I didn't know what had hit me and Audrey didn't know what she'd hit, but then she saw me, smiled and shook her finger in front of my face, as if I'd been a naughty boy. I *had* been a naughty boy. I'd been so focused on the camera that I'd drifted out of position. I took the regulator out of my mouth and smiled sheepishly, then came close and kissed her. I was about to try to plant a little smooch on her ass, which is a little thing we did, but she unhitched the sled, inflated the lift bag, and shot toward the surface.

I went down to retrieve the sled, and to let Pascal know that everything was under control—I knew he'd be worried. That descent was going to increase my decompression time, but that was okay with me. I'd been responsible for the aborted dive, and I wasn't looking forward to the tongue-lashing I was going to get from the crew. I figured if I stayed in the water long enough, they might forget what an idiot I'd been.

I thought wrong. When I finally surfaced, three hours later, they all tore into me with undisguised glee.

"*¡Pipín, anormal!*" they shouted. Yes, I was "subnormal" and an idiot. It was a word that often popped out of my mouth when I got mad.

"*¡Súper anormal!*"

Okay. I'm sorry. String me up.

That night, Audrey slept like a rock, and in the morning she awoke full of vim and vigor. We talked about the coming dive and ended up deciding, together, that she should try for 151 meters. That would show Umberto Pelizzari! A woman, a relative newcomer to the sport, would shatter his record.

That day, at the site, there was the usual nervous tension. But Audrey was as imperturbable as ever. By the time the countdown began, she was so deeply in the zone she didn't even see me blow her a good-bye kiss.

Pascal swam down to the end of the line. I positioned myself at the hundred-meter mark.

About a minute after I was in position, Audrey came shooting past. She was in total control, both on the way down and on the way up, and I was thrilled. But less than twenty minutes later, while Pascal and I were hanging on the line, waiting to decompress, Tata swam down with his slate. He wrote out the number 143. Damn, we had screwed up again! We must have measured the line incorrectly.

I was sure Audrey was going to be upset, but when it was finally safe for me to surface she just laughed and hugged me.

"You're not mad?" I said, incredulous.

"No."

"We really messed up," I said, feeling guilty. "I don't know how it happened. But you were very close."

"It's fine," she said. "It felt great. It was easy. I could have kept going forever."

At that point, my guilt gave way to another feeling altogether: confidence. She was brimming with confidence, which only fueled my own confidence.

"How easy was it?" I asked.

"Pretty easy," she said.

"So why not break my record?" I suggested. "Why not go for one sixty-three? If you do that now, you won't have any trouble at all on October twelfth, when we do it for the books."

"Gee, I don't know," she said, nibbling at her nails. "I don't know if I'm ready."

"You just said it was easy!" I replied.

"It is easy. *Physically.* I'm talking about psychologically. I'm not sure I like competing with you. It's never been about competition for me. It's always been about challenging myself."

"Let's be realistic," I said. "I haven't had a record in three years. I've choked a couple of times. I feel like one of those old cars you see on the streets of Havana: I'm still running, but I've got way too many miles on this old body."

"It's a nice old body," she said.

"You're on a roll," I continued, on a roll of my own. "You've never had a single diving-related problem. Nothing. Zip. Zero. If you make it, I make it. You'd be doing it for both of us."

"You mean that?" she asked.

"Yes," I said. "And like I told you: I'm going to break one hundred eighty meters by the end of the year, so don't worry about breaking my record. It won't be for long."

Audrey took a moment. She seemed as if she were about to start ventilating, but I guess she was only taking a deep, bracing breath to steady herself. "Okay," she said. "You think I'm ready and I think I'm ready, so why not?"

I kissed her.

"Let's go back to the room," she said. "I want to call my parents."

Audrey called her parents every other day. Anne Marie was in Mexico, where the family was stationed, but Jean Pierre had just left for France on a business-related meeting, and he wasn't expected back for a few days.

Over the years, Anne Marie had made an effort to attend all of Audrey's important dives, but this time she couldn't make it. Jean Pierre, on the other hand, had made it clear long ago that he wasn't equipped to watch Audrey risk her life for the sake of a sport he didn't really understand.

When Audrey told them she was going to try to beat my record, they were less than thrilled. There were calls back and forth, to Mom in Mexico City and to Dad in Paris.

"Why so deep?" Jean Pierre said. "Are you being pressured to do this?"

"No, no," she said. "Pipín and I talked about this at length. I want to do it. And you know me: no one forces me to do anything I don't want to do."

Anne Marie paid more attention to the sport, and followed stories about it more closely. She had just read about a German free diver in Aruba who had tried for the world record, blacked out near the surface, and inexplicably lost his ability to speak. It was clear there had been some brain damage.

"Mom, please don't worry," Audrey said. "I did a hundred forty-three meters and it felt easier than my hundred-thirty-meter record. And if anything doesn't feel right, if I have any doubts at all, I'll cancel."

Audrey moments before a dive. That's me next to her, ready to set her loose.

On October 4, we laid out 165 meters' worth of line. This was two meters more than we needed, but I didn't want to risk coming up short. Audrey didn't know about the two additional meters, but before she went in the water I took her aside to reiterate what I had been telling her from the start: if at any point something didn't feel right, I wanted her to hit the brakes and call it a day.

"I know," she said. "I'm fine."

The dive went flawlessly. She shot past me at the halfway mark, looking very relaxed, and shot back up with lightning speed. I was thrilled, and I wanted to swim up and take her in my arms and hug her, but I had a couple of hours of decompression ahead of me. Pascal worked his way up and joined me, and a moment later Tata swam down with his slate. He wrote out the number "166." We were amazed. He nodded happily and indicated that Audrey was on the boat, feeling like a million bucks.

By the time I surfaced, she was in great spirits, joking around with Carlos and the rest of the crew.

"You broke my record!" I yelled, grabbing her and twirling her around.

"Yes, I did!" she shouted back. "Let's see you try to get it back in December!"

This had been a practice dive, of course, and we still had to make it official, but everyone was pumped, especially Audrey.

"It was great," she said when I asked her how she felt. "Couldn't have been better."

"*Pipín, socio,*" Tata said, shaking his head from side to side. "How does it feel to get beaten, and by a *woman?*"

Everyone laughed, and I laughed right along with them. Under normal circumstances, I would have responded like a typical macho Latino, which is how many people see me. But not this time. This time I felt like crying. I was so proud of Audrey I was coming apart at the seams.

"This isn't just any woman," I said, putting my arm around her. "This is Audrey Mestre. Part mermaid, part angel, and all mine!"

*   *   *

That night, at dinner, Audrey sat next to Matt Briseno. Although I didn't find out about this till much later, she told him that she had felt "a little weird" during the course of her dive. She didn't say it was a bad feeling, only that it was different, and Matt didn't think anything of it, so he didn't share it with me. After all, Audrey remained in fine high spirits.

For the rest of the week, I kept hearing the digs. "Hey, coach, how does it feel to be number two?" Or, "Hey, old man, think you still got it?"

It was a little rough on the ego, admittedly, but I handled it. I logged on to our website and updated our fans on Audrey's spectacular day, and I even invited them to try to predict the exact depth and time of her forthcoming dive. E-mails poured in from around the globe. A woman in Canada said she'd do 165 meters in two and a half minutes flat; a fan from Mexico expected 166 meters in two minutes, thirty-eight seconds; a German hoped to see 170 meters in two minutes, forty-five seconds.

While I was still logged on, I took the time to remind everyone that I was planning another dive of my own, and that I intended to prove, once and for all, that I was King of the Deep. That may have been my insecurity showing: I wasn't trying to steal Audrey's thunder, but I wanted everyone to know that I wasn't out of the game.

What can I tell you? I'm human.

For the next few days, we took it easy. Audrey was ahead of schedule, and we didn't want to overdo her time in the water. She did a little weight lifting, a little running, some breathing exercises and daily meditation, and she treated the whole thing like a vacation.

The crew also enjoyed their time off. They rode horses on the beach or raced around in the water on rented Jet Skis.

I, on the other hand, found it almost impossible to relax. I seldom relax on these trips. There is too much to keep track of, and I tend to get stressed over every detail, and that's exactly what I did. I got stressed about weather, time, money, even the future.

Audrey, however, remained happily stress-free. The only time she ever did anything that seemed a little odd was over dinner one night. There was a fanatical diver at the resort who had come along as an observer, and he talked tirelessly and incessantly about diving. Records, techniques, equipment. Blah blah blah. He was monomaniacal.

"Hey," Audrey snapped at him. "Can we talk about something besides diving?"

There was a lot of bite in her voice, which was unlike her. But I couldn't blame her. The guy was getting on everyone's nerves.

By October 9, having had enough time to analyze and overanalyze the coming event, I began to think that we were selling ourselves short. I didn't understand why Audrey couldn't shoot for 170 meters. It was such a nice, clean, round number, and no one—*no one,* male or female—had ever even come close.

Audrey could do it. She had managed 166 meters without a hitch. Another four meters was within her grasp.

When I mentioned it to her, she was immediately game. She said she'd give it a shot on Wednesday, during the dress rehearsal, and again on Saturday, the day of the big dive.

On Wednesday, as promised, she took the plunge.

She shot past me, her ponytail trailing behind her like an auburn exclamation mark, hit her mark, then flew back behind the lift bag. When she was about fifteen to twenty meters from the surface, however, she let go of the lift bag. Tata raced down to see what was wrong, but it was a false alarm. Audrey felt so good that she wanted to swim the rest of the way to the surface. When she got there, she sucked air into her empty lungs, looked at all the smiling faces on the boat, and flashed a confident thumbs-up.

The woman was unstoppable.

Tata swam over and unstrapped one of her depth gauges, He held it aloft as Carlos snapped a photo. One hundred and seventy meters. There it was, for all the world to see.

Audrey had willed herself through 18 atmospheres of pressure, enduring 264 pounds per square inch, to go deeper than any human had ever gone before. And on the return trip, she'd had enough energy and confidence to cover the final meters under her own steam.

It was truly awe-inspiring.

"I'm very proud of you," Pascal told Audrey that evening.

"Please," she said. "Let's not talk about it anymore. It's not official yet, and I don't want to jinx it, and I'm frankly sick and tired of talking about diving."

But I wasn't sick of talking about diving. I'd been obsessed with it all my life, and I was suddenly more obsessed than ever.

"Audrey," I said. "Why not go for one eighty-two? Six hundred feet even."

"You're crazy," Wiky said. "Then what'll you aim for in December?"

"Hell," I said. "If Audrey can do this shit, I can do two hundred."

The table went silent. I wish I could say that I'd been drinking, that it was just liquor talking, but I was stone-cold sober. It wasn't liquor talking. It was my ego.

Carlos looked over at me, visibly displeased. "What are you calling 'shit,' *socio*?" he said, trying to keep the edge out of his voice. "Audrey's gone deeper than you've ever gone."

I didn't say anything. I know I should have apologized, but I was embarrassed enough already. Dinner wound down and we moved to the bar by the pool. And *still* I couldn't let it go. I told Carlos, again, that Audrey could break 180, and he told me, *again,* that I was getting dangerously ambitious.

"You're crazy," he said. "You're burning too many meters. There'll be nothing left to try. Leave it alone."

But I refused to leave it alone. I knew Pascal could handle 182 meters, and I knew we'd need another safety diver at 130. It would of course have to be someone who had trained with Trimix, someone like me. It's tricky, but it didn't worry me. At extreme depths, regular compressed air feels almost like honey—it's harder to breathe. That's why divers mix it up whenever they go below 50 meters. The combination of oxygen, nitrogen, and helium is much lighter. What's more, by reducing the percentage of nitrogen, you're less likely to get nitrogen narcosis on the way back, those so-called bends. But there's a price you pay. Pascal had to dive with five tanks, three on his back and two clipped to his sides, each with a slightly different mixture. He had to breathe from five different regulators, according to his depth. If he took air from the wrong one at the wrong point, he risked death.

It was also expensive: a whopping $1,200 per dive.

Still, I could do it. I'd been down on Trimix hundreds of times.

"How about if I'm the guy at the bottom of the line?" I told Carlos.

"That's ridiculous," Carlos said. "You can't do everything. Don't be such a control freak."

"It's my wife down there," I said. "I want to be with her. I know free diving better than anyone. If Pascal makes me the right mix and recalculates the dive tables, I'll be fine."

"It's not that simple," Wiky piped up. "You don't have the technical experience for a dive like that."

"What are you talking about?" I shot back. "I've gone down on Trimix dozens of times!"

"Let's think about this for a moment," Pascal said. He was always such a diplomat.

"No," Audrey said. "Let's not think about it. I don't want Pipín at the bottom. It'll take him hours to decompress." She took my hand in hers. "I want him waiting for me up top, with a big victory kiss."

By the end of the evening, we reached a compromise. Pascal would be the deepest safety diver, as always, and I would stick to the original plan and wait for Audrey on the surface.

As for the dive itself, everyone thought that Audrey should not try to go beyond 171 meters.

"Audrey?" I asked. "What do you think?"

"I think that's good," she said. "One seventy-one is good."

A practice dive before Audrey's fatal dive.

"You've got serious *cojones,* girl," Tata said. That's the ultimate compliment from a Cubano. You've got balls; you've got guts; you're fearless.

To be completely honest, I was still fixated on one eighty. But for once in my life I decided to listen to the crew. "Okay," I said. "One seventy-one it is."

Audrey and I walked back to our room, hand in hand. I looked out at the ocean, bathed in shadows, and at the waves crashing on the beach.

Something didn't feel right about it, but I had no idea what it was.

On October 11, the night before the dive, Audrey called her mother in Mexico City.

"I won't have time to call you in the morning," she said, "but we'll talk right after the dive." She told her that she had just bought a pair of plane tickets for her and Jean Pierre, who were going to be spending Christmas with us. "We're going to get a big tree and put lights up all over the house," she said. "And I want to do some redecorating, so you'll have to help me pick out the paint and stuff, okay?"

When she got off the phone, I asked Audrey how she was feeling. "She's great," she said. "They're really looking forward to spending Christmas in Miami."

"I meant *you,*" I said. "How are *you* feeling?"

"Never better," she said.

I slept badly that night, and woke up abruptly, bathed in sweat. I realized I'd been dreaming. In my dream, I had been diving, and had surfaced to a violent storm. I got the impression that Chango, the Santeria god of hurricanes, tornadoes, and lightning, was angry with me, but I didn't understand why. I was swimming in a dark, churning sea, in a torrential downpour, and bolts of lightning kept cracking across sky.

Now I remembered that Chango had spoken to me in the dream. He told me that he was angry. I always paid homage to Olokun, he said, but I never once showed him any respect at all.

I was confused. As a child, I'd been told that God lives in heaven. But I could never visualize God in heaven. For me, Olokun was God, and he lived in the depths. Whenever I was in the water, I felt closer to God, to Olokun, but I had never given much thought to Chango.

I heard the thrum of rain against the windows and got up and looked outside. It was storming, and I saw a distant flash of lightning. I went back to bed and looked at Audrey. She was fast asleep.

When she woke up, I said nothing about the dream, and Audrey told me that she wasn't hungry and that I should go to breakfast on my own. I passed a knot of reporters on the way to the dining room, raced through a typically subdued breakfast, then hurried back to the room with a few filched items in my pockets.

"What are you hiding there?" Audrey said with an impish smile, setting her book down on her chest.

I showed her: a banana, a few slices of mango, some honey.

"Who's that for?" she asked. "Olokun?"

"Yes," I said. "Him, and the other one."

I left the offering by the window and returned to Audrey's side and sat on the bed next to her. She was reading something about ancient Egypt. She'd been reading about ancient Egypt ever since our trip to the Red Sea.

"I need you to wear something red today," I said.

"Why?" she said.

"For Chango. He came to me in a dream last night. He's angry. Red is his color."

"That sounds right," Audrey said with a smile. "Red for anger."

I found one of my red T-shirts and ripped a small strip off the bottom and gave it to her. "Tie that around your wrist before you come to the site," I said.

I kissed her and left her there and hurried through the drizzle to see the crew, but I stopped on my way to tell the assembled reporters that everything would go ahead as planned, if a little behind schedule.

I met the guys on the beach. They were glum, mostly on account of the weather. We talked about postponing the dive but I had already decided against it, so we went off to load the catamaran.

The gear never seemed to end: fins, masks, snorkels, buoyancy compensator backpacks, weight belts, wet suits. Cameras. Toolboxes. A cooler. A case of water. Boxes of PowerBars. Next came the scuba tanks, almost two dozen of them, including five for the decompression line.

It was muggy. I used my T-shirt to dry the nose pads on my glasses. I looked at my watch: 11 A.M. Our original dive time.

"We've got to hurry up," I said, turning to look at Carlos. "Bring Audrey out at two P.M. ¡*Vámonos!*"

I checked the beach to make sure we hadn't left anything behind, then hopped back into the catamaran and off we went.

Pascal was on the port side of the boat, lining up his five tanks. He marked each one with duct tape, to keep track of the five different mixes.

I turned to find Matt and Tata fiddling with the sled's decoupling pin. "I'll take care of that," I said. "You guys did it wrong the other day."

I tested the pin, twice, then went over every inch of the sled. It was my latest model. It was threaded with a thinner, vinyl-coated cable, to reduce friction. The cable was spooled around two posts. We had used a Sharpie pen to mark off 171 meters on the cable. I carefully examined the lift bag and found no rips or tears. I detached the unit from the weighted stage—the lift bag and the small, yellow pony tank—to make sure the pin mechanism was working properly. It was.

I turned and saw Kim on the far side of the boat. He was wearing his bifocals and tapping away at the keys of his laptop. He looked excited. Today was one for the books.

I went over to check the cameras. I made sure they were loaded and snapped a couple of frames on each one.

Within fifteen minutes, we had reached the site. We dropped anchor and got to work rigging the sled. That whole, unwieldy business. Using the boom as a crane. Swinging it out over the water. Lowering the sled into position.

And even now, as I write this, I'm reliving every moment, as I've relived it a thousand times since:

I'm in the water now. I'm reaching for the yellow pony tank under the lift bag. I give the valve a twist. I hear that telltale hiss and feel a puff of air against my hand and listen to the crinkling of the lift bag. I see myself, almost in close-up, screwing the valve shut, nice and tight.

I turn to Tata, in the water next to me, and Tata hollers up to the boat. "The yellow tank—it's full?"

The answer comes back: "Yes."

Remembering all the rest of it. The way we fed the line into the water, 171 meters' worth. The leaky camera housing. The screwdriver. The clamp. Trouble with the focus. I remember the boats arriving, crowding me with their noise and smoke.

And then suddenly it's two o'clock and Audrey's there, arriving with Carlos. Audrey in a black T-shirt over her bikini. My wife. My angel. My savior.

I get out of the water. Kiss her. Tell her how beautiful she looks. She goes off to prepare, eager to get the show on the road. I get back in the water to finish fixing the camera. But it's taking too damn long, so I ask Tata to send for Audrey. "She needs to start her warm-ups," I tell him.

The boats keep coming, puttering and spewing.

"*¡Poquito espacio!*" I'm hollering, irritated. "A little room!"

I see the divers gearing up. Pascal slips into his long underwear; sprinkling baby powder into the sleeves and legs of his dry suit; squeezes in. He's going to be spending several hours in the water and needs plenty of insulation.

I finally finish fixing the camera and join Audrey for a final warm-up dive. She looks centered; relaxed. We swim over to the sled and she lifts herself onto the crossbar.

God, she's beautiful.

I turn to look behind me. Pascal is sitting on the pontoon; Kim is helping him into his three-tank backpack. When Pascal lowers himself into the water, Kim hands him the two remaining tanks. Pascal clips them to his shoulder straps and fiddles with his bouquet of regulators. He tests the two flashlights strapped to either side of his head.

Practicing yoga in Cabo San Lucas.

Wiky and the other diver clomp up to the side of the boat, geared up and ready to roll. It's showtime, folks.

I turn back to look at Audrey.

"All good?" I ask.

All good. All good. It's the last thing I'll ever say to her.

Then the scene I've played in my mind's eye more times than I can count:

The way she half-smiled, not answering, and turned her attention to the horizon, getting further focused, more deeply zoned. The way she began to ventilate, inhaling and exhaling with mounting force, each breath deeper and more powerful than the preceding one.

The dozen boats, edging closer. Me, trying to wave them back without success. The talking, the laughter, the clicking and whirring of the cameras.

I look at Audrey again. My Audrey. *Together Forever.*

But she's already inside that soundproof room in her head, her eyes hooded and distant, her breathing rhythmic.

Then the countdown begins and the divers are in the water and even the spectators have grown quiet.

And then, "Zero minutes!" Carlos says. *"Cero minutos."*

Zero minutes. We are out of time. Out of time. That's what I have left: nothing.

Audrey looks at me and I see a hint of that impish smile in her eyes, distant now, turned inward. One final, protracted breath—and she's gone.

The cable vibrating in my hand. Audrey slowed by that touch of air in the lift bag, but still ahead of schedule.

Carlos, excited: "She's good, she's good. She's making good time."

All of it coming back:

How I pictured her down there, as calm as a safecracker, disconnecting herself from the sled and opening the valve on the pony tank, to fill the lift bag. She wasn't even feeling the urge to breathe yet. She didn't need to breathe. If anything, the euphoria was hitting her at that very moment. There were times down there, at that very juncture, when I felt like laughing out loud.

Now she was on her way. I imagined her turning to look at Pascal, smiling, and flashing a thumbs-up. She'd be inflating the bag by now, and by now she'd be shooting toward me, coming back to me, my Audrey.

But where was she? I was still hanging on to the cable, and I didn't feel a thing. Then suddenly, a faint vibration. It was Audrey, fifty-five stories down, Audrey on her way home, and I was overcome with relief.

At precisely two and a half minutes, I lowered my goggled face into the water, expecting to see the rising bubbles that would announce her arrival. Tata dove down to twenty meters, but quickly came back up, looking alarmed, and shook his head. There was no sign of her. Nothing. Nothing but the line disappearing into the blackness.

Three minutes had passed.

Where in God's name was Audrey? Her longest No Limits dive had *never* exceeded three minutes. What was keeping her? Then we saw the bubbles of the lift bag below us. It was not ascending at its usual speed.

"Here she comes," I thought, relieved. But she wasn't holding on to it. She wasn't there at all. The lift bag was like a riderless horse, loping home on instinct.

Oh, Jesus God. Help me.

Why had she let go of the lift bag? Had the sled jammed? Had narcosis clouded her judgment?

No, wait! Everything was fine. She was down there with Pascal, breathing. They'd had to abort. No big deal. Tomorrow was another day.

Four minutes and thirty seconds.

And no Audrey. Because Audrey had to stay down to decompress, right? She was breathing from Pascal's regulator; she had no choice.

What the hell was I saying? What was I trying to talk myself into? Or out of?

My heart was thumping in my ears. I couldn't take the not-knowing. I needed to be down there.

I noticed the people on the boats, dancing and singing, oblivious.

"Give me my tank!" I said. "Give me my tank, damn it!"

Five minutes had elapsed. Kim handed me the backpack I'd prepared and Tata helped me into it. I shot down the line like an arrow, kicking as hard as I could, and passed Wiky and the other safety diver.

There was still no sign of Audrey. I kept going. When I hit ninety meters, I saw bubbles. And there she was! She was with Pascal, her trusted friend, her savior, and they were breathing together.

But as I got closer, I saw that she wasn't breathing at all. She was unconscious. Pascal was frantic, struggling to wrap an orange marker buoy around her wrist. I raced closer. Pink foam was coming out of her mouth. I could see her eyes beyond the mask, open and unseeing.

Oh, Jesus God. No.

I had to get her out of there. I had to get her up into the air and light.

Pascal handed her to me. She felt so light, as light as a child. I turned her around, facing away from me, and slipped an arm under both of hers. Her head lolled against my chest, just below my chin. Her back was pressed to my stomach. I kicked for the surface.

More than seven minutes had passed.

We're going to make it. Everything is going to be all right.

But what the hell had happened, damn it? Why hadn't Pascal brought her up? I knew he was at his absolute decompression limit, and that if he climbed another meter or two he would have been writing his own death sentence. But where was our ninety-meter man? I knew he didn't have Trimix in his tanks, but so what—hadn't he seen the empty sled limping toward the surface? Hadn't he seen the bubbles?

Something had happened in that no-man's-land between Pascal and Wiky, and I had no idea what it was.

At fifty meters, I saw Tata racing down to meet me. He grabbed my weight belt and helped pull me toward the surface and we broke through together.

Eight minutes and thirty-eight seconds.

I clamped my mouth over Audrey's mouth and tried to fill her with air. There was no other way. If we didn't get her back now, if we didn't get the blood flowing, she wouldn't make it.

"*¡Aspira!*" I said, my voice rising. "Breathe!"

Carlos and the others took her from my hands and lifted her onto the pontoon. She had a pulse! She gasped faintly a couple times.

"Audrey, we're here," I shouted, my voice cracking.

Pink foam kept oozing out of her mouth and nose. That meant there was water in her lungs. We wiped it away with a towel, but it kept coming. There was so much of it I could hardly bear to look.

Carlos tried to give her mouth-to-mouth, but he couldn't clear her airway. We had no intubation kit or defibrillator aboard. We had to get her ashore. I stroked her forehead and spoke into her ear.

"*Fight!*" I said. If I could just penetrate her mind, her powerful mind: "Fight, damn you! Fight like you've always fought!"

Tata was crying, a couple of people on the boat had fainted, and the cameras—the goddamn cameras—just kept rolling.

"Her pulse is fading," Carlos said. He had his fingers on her carotid artery. "Let's move."

We transferred Audrey to a launch and roared off. Her eyes were still open, but fixed and dilated, unresponsive to the light. One minute into the trip, she stopped breathing altogether. One of the paramedics began giving her mouth-to-mouth. Matt held her head, and the foam kept coming, followed now by a thick green fluid.

I couldn't look.

A minute later, Audrey's heart stopped. Matt zipped open her wet suit and tried chest compressions. Nothing worked.

A second paramedic tried to feed her oxygen, placing a tube in her mouth, and he kept trying until we reached the beach. Oxygen, mouth-to-mouth, chest compressions. *Nothing* worked.

It had taken us five minutes to reach shore. With help from patrol guards on the beach, we lifted Audrey onto a chaise cushion and raced across the sand and up the steps and past the pool, to the hotel infirmary.

A laborer was working inside, painting the walls, and all the equipment had been shoved to one side. "Get out!" someone yelled at him.

We laid Audrey on the cot. The hotel doctor hurried in with a nurse, and a moment later a white-haired man raced inside in his bathing suit and identified himself as a doctor. "I saw you rushing past the pool," he said. "Can I help?"

But he couldn't help. Not him or the hotel doctor or any of the rest of us, and certainly not me. More oxygen. More chest compressions. A frantic search for the defibrillator. It was pandemonium.

Then an ambulance arrived and we piled Audrey into it and raced to the hospital, still trying to force air into her lungs. I held on to her hand as we careened around corners, tires screeching and siren wailing.

It took thirty minutes to reach the medical facility at La Romana. At this point, it had been more than an hour since the accident, and they told us they were sorry, but there was nothing they could do. We knew that, but we didn't want to hear it.

"I'm her husband," I yelled. "Do something, damn you!"

They took her inside. They tried shocking her back to life with the paddles, but it was no use. Her heart, the heart of a lion, had stopped beating.

"I'm sorry," the nurse said.

I didn't want to hear that, either. Those two words had never carried so much weight. But now the nurse couldn't take them back, and I'd heard them, and they would stay with me for the rest of my life.

I'm sorry I'm sorry I'm sorry.

I stumbled out of the room, collapsed in a chair, and buried my face in my hands.

Audrey was gone.

We went back to the hotel in a daze, leaving Audrey's body behind at the hospital. We'd been told there would be an autopsy. It was required by law.

We didn't speak a word during the entire ride. I think we were afraid to acknowledge what had just happened. Blindly, I followed Carlos through the lobby, feeling lost and numb and hopelessly empty, and as we walked into his room the phone began to ring. Matt Briseno answered it.

"Hello?" he said, and listened for a moment. "Just a minute, please." He turned to look at me, but he had trouble meeting my eyes. "It's Audrey's mother," he said.

"Can you talk to her?" I asked Carlos. "I can't do it."

Carlos took the phone. Anne Marie was eager to hear how the dive had gone. She had expected Audrey to call by now. Did she set a world record?

"No," Carlos said. "There's—there's been an accident."

"What happened?" she said, not fully understanding him. "You've postponed it?"

"No," he said. "It's Audrey."

"She's okay, isn't she?"

"No," Carlos said. "I'm sorry. We couldn't save her."

Anne Marie fell apart, and Carlos did his best to calm her down. He said he was sorry, that we didn't know what had gone wrong, or why, and that we were still trying to figure out exactly what had happened. He then turned and handed me the phone. "I think you should talk to her," he said.

I took the phone. "Anne Marie?"

She was sobbing. I waited for her to catch her breath, then I asked her to please get on the next plane. "I need you here," I said.

When I got off the phone, I felt intensely claustrophobic. We left the room and went down to the beach, past the oblivious tourists, and ran into Kim. He was on his way back to the dive site with some food for Pascal, who was still underwater, decompressing, and who remained in the dark.

He hugged me, then turned to Carlos. "What should I tell Pascal?"

"Nothing," Carlos said. "Wait till he's out of the water."

At dusk, Kim returned with the others, and we gathered on the beach, where we had been waiting for them. Everyone was in shock, and I felt so fragile I could barely raise my head, but we were all desperate to know what had happened. We needed to focus on something other than Audrey's death; on the details; on the questions. If we could do that, we wouldn't have to deal with it, and for a short time we could put off acknowledging it—for a short time we could pretend it had never happened.

Nobody understood what had gone wrong. Three days earlier, Audrey had done an almost identical dive without a hitch. Now we were sitting in a semicircle, a group of devastated people, trying to make sense of something that would never make sense. We were studying Kim's data, which included a graph of the dive. The descent had gone flawlessly. Wiky remembered Audrey shooting past at ninety meters, the point at which she switched to wet equalization, ahead of schedule. At the bottom, everything went like clockwork, too. For the first few seconds, anyway. Pascal watched as Audrey drew out the pin, separating the weighted portion of the sled, and that too went without a hitch.

But then Audrey unscrewed the valve on the pony tank and the lift bag failed to inflate. In fact, it actually sank a little.

"It looked like no air was coming out of the tank," Pascal said.

No air in the tank? That couldn't be possible. I had checked the tank. It was full. I had opened the valve and felt the telltale hiss and even heard the crinkle of the lift bag as a burst of air found its way inside. I *knew* there was air in the tank. I even remembered thinking, later, that that little burst of air I'd released, in testing it, to make sure it was full, might have slowed Audrey's descent.

"Did you *check* the pony tank?" Carlos asked me.

"Yes," I said. *"Yes."*

Tata spoke up. He said he had called up to the boat, to ask if the pony tank had been filled, "And somebody said yes."

"Who?" Carlos asked.

"I don't know," Tata said.

"I heard it, too," I said. But I didn't know who it was, either.

Everyone looked at everyone else. No one knew who had spoken up earlier. And no one spoke up at that moment.

The fact is, the responsibility for filling the tank didn't fall on the shoulders of any single member of the team. We were a *team,* and that's how we always operated. One day I made sure the tanks were filled. Another day it was Tata. Another Wiky or Carlos or Matt. It was the way we had always done it, and it had never failed us. Until now.

Carlos turned his attention back to Pascal. "What happened next?" he said.

"I swam over to help Audrey," Pascal said. "She opened her eyes briefly, but I saw no panic. She tried to push the sled upward, but it stalled. So I tried to push it, too."

According to Kim's graph, Pascal and Audrey spent seventeen seconds struggling with the sled, which barely climbed two meters. Pascal then used one of his regulators to pump air into the lift bag, and it moved a little farther up, to 165 meters.

The next thirty seconds were critical. Pascal continued to add air, but the bag barely moved. Audrey had been at the bottom for a full minute, and it had been two minutes and forty-two seconds since she'd taken her last breath. She should have been seconds from home, and she was barely seven meters from the bottom.

"She didn't ask for air," Pascal said. "She appeared calm. We've always had the same agreement. Audrey would ask to breathe from a regulator only as a last resort. She didn't want to take that risk."

For the next eighteen seconds, according to the data, Audrey began to rise, haltingly, at about half her normal speed, but the bag stalled again at the three-minute mark. By that time, I should have been holding her in my arms, celebrating on the surface, but she was 153 meters below me, an eternity away.

Just before the four-minute mark, Audrey reached 120 meters. But according to the depth gauge, as recorded on Kim's computers, she suddenly stopped climbing and began to drop.

"She'd been holding her breath for four minutes," Kim said. "I'm assuming that she lost consciousness and lost her grip on the lift bag."

In Cabo San Lucas for my commemorative dive.
That's Jim Cameron behind the camera, on the right.

She was at the 120-meter mark. This was where Cédric would have been waiting for her; Cédric her guardian angel. But we had decided not to put another safety diver in his place. Audrey was almost precisely halfway between Pascal and Wiky, all alone.

"I was below her," Pascal said. "Coming up slowly, at my usual ascent rate. Suddenly I saw her drifting off the lift-bag. She was falling toward me at a strange angle, almost like a leaf, and the sled was slowly going up without her."

Within fifteen seconds, Pascal stopped Audrey's fall, literally catching her. She was no longer breathing, so he couldn't put a regulator into her mouth. He inflated his vest and began to carry her up, holding on to her with his right arm and pulling himself along the cable with his left. He needed to reach Wiky fast, and he kept climbing—though of course he knew that if he didn't stop to decompress the results could be fatal.

After one minute and 55 seconds, he had reached the 90-meter mark, but Wiky wasn't there. Six minutes had elapsed since Audrey had taken her last breath.

"At that point, it was life and death for me," Pascal said, his voice cracking with emotion. "I had already missed one decompression stop at one hundred meters. I couldn't keep going. I have a wife and daughter. I couldn't take the risk."

Pascal didn't understand why Wiky wasn't at his post, and neither did we. Was he narked out of his mind? He'd been breathing regular air at 90 meters, though a mix was recommended at any point below 50. Hadn't Wiky seen the lift bag go by, without Audrey on it? How could he have missed it—it was moving very slowly. We were all staring at Wiky.

"No, no," he protested, near tears. "You don't understand. I saw the empty lift bag. But six minutes had gone by. It was obvious the dive had been aborted. I began to return to the surface. I figured Audrey was below, with Pascal, and that they were going to decompress together. I didn't want to think about any other possibility . . . I didn't want to think she might be gone."

After climbing toward the surface, Wiky couldn't have returned to that depth without risking the bends, and he didn't actually think there was any reason for him to go back. The dive had been aborted; it wouldn't have been the first time.

Meanwhile, Pascal waited at the 90-meter mark for one minute and three seconds. It felt like an eternity. He tied the buoy around Audrey and began to inflate it, thinking he would have to release her and let her float to the top. That's when I arrived: seven minutes and three seconds into it.

Audrey had been unconscious for more than three minutes.

"She seemed very peaceful," Pascal told me. "I didn't want to look at her face. I thought I'd fall apart. When I handed her to you, I tried to tell myself there was still hope. I was just glad you were there—I was glad she was with you."

It took me another minute and 35 seconds to get Audrey to the surface. She had been underwater for eight minutes and 38 seconds.

At that rate of ascent, I could have died. And as I sat there with the others, trying to figure out exactly what had happened, trying to understand where we went wrong, I found myself wishing I *had* died.

For a long time, no one spoke. The waves churned against the sand and retreated. In the near distance, we could hear the festive, piped-in music. I looked up at the sky. It was a clear night, and the heavens were ablaze with stars. I had met Audrey on a night like this. Now she was gone. I couldn't understand it. And I didn't want to accept it.

I closed my eyes and rubbed my head, then stood and walked down the beach, into the shadows. I wanted to be alone. But I was already alone. I had never been more alone in my life.

↓

Chapter_ NINE:

BURIAL AT SEA

Audrey takes in the sunset in Miami.

When I got back to the hotel room, hours later, I unclenched my fists and found I'd been carrying Audrey's jewelry in my hands. In one hand, I had her titanium wedding band and an antique ring that her grandmother had given her. In the other, a toe ring, six diamond stud-earrings, and her Mayan necklace. I couldn't for the life of me remember how I had ended up with these things, but I imagine someone at the hospital had given them to me.

I set them down on the dresser and noticed Audrey's slippers by the side of the unmade bed. For a moment, I thought I was asleep, that I was dreaming, and that the dive hadn't taken place yet. But it was such a horrible dream that I knew I had to call off the dive. The moment I woke up, I would tell Audrey about the dream, and I would explain why I felt compelled to cancel everything.

But then I realized I wasn't dreaming.

Audrey was dead. She was twenty-eight years old, in the prime of life, and she was *dead*.

I left the room. I didn't want to be with anyone, but I was afraid to be alone. As I shut the door behind me, I saw the Do Not Disturb sign hanging from the knob. That's why the bed remained unmade. Audrey was superstitious. On the day of a dive, she always wanted to return to the room exactly as she had left it.

I wandered through the lobby and out to the pool. Everyone was sitting around, looking miserable, emptied out, and they came over to comfort me and offer their condolences. I scarcely heard them. *I'm so sorry. She's at peace. She died doing what she loved best.* It was all so meaningless. She wasn't at peace. She was gone.

Somebody slipped a glass of juice into my hand, and I sat down and drank it, and tried not to notice the way they were all looking at me. The sad eyes. The pursed lips. The gestures of support.

I drank my juice and tried not to think of Audrey, but I could think of nothing else. It was like a bad movie: I kept seeing her in flashback. The day we met, in Cabo. Playing with the dolphins at Roatán. Our sunset wedding on the dock of our home, with the sky over Miami turning a hue of lavender I'd never seen before.

Suddenly I was very tired. I felt as if I were looking at the world from a great distance. The voices gurgled. Everything sounded as if it were underwater.

"Come on, *socio*. Let me walk you back to your room." It was Tata. He reached for my arm and helped me to my feet.

"I feel weird, man."

"Yeah. We put a sedative in your drink. To help you sleep."

I was too tired to protest.

Tata walked me upstairs and dropped me on the bed.

"Somebody will be right outside your door," he said. "If you need anything, holler."

The next morning, a woman from the resort drove Carlos and me back out to La Romana. The facility had no refrigeration, and we had to transfer Audrey's body to the morgue in Santo Domingo. She was still in her yellow wet suit, and Carlos had had the wherewithal to bring some of her clothes, but I couldn't change her. I couldn't look at her like that.

"Okay," Carlos said, his voice breaking. "I'll do it."

The woman from the resort could see how difficult this was for both of us and offered to take care of it.

"Thank you," Carlos said. "It means the world to us."

"Don't mention it," she said.

When she was done, we were told that we needed a death certificate, but the doctor wasn't there. So someone called him at home and we waited for him to show up, and then we rented a van to take Audrey's body to Santo Domingo.

The next thing I know, Carlos and I are at the local police precinct, in a small room, talking to the investigating officer. *Did Audrey seem depressed? Is there any reason she might have wanted to harm herself? Is it possible someone wanted to harm her?*

No. Nothing like that. That's crazy. Audrey was happy. She loved life. And everybody loved Audrey.

I felt like I was in the middle of a bad television show. I was being interrogated by a cop who would never understand what I was feeling, and I was trying not to cry. I didn't want to cry. Audrey's death still hadn't fully registered, and if I cried there'd be no going back.

"I'm sorry," the police officer said. "I know this is difficult, but I had to ask you these questions."

"I understand," I said, but I really didn't understand.

Then it was time to drive to the airport to pick up Audrey's parents. I didn't think I could face them, but Carlos said, rightly, that I didn't have a choice.

Jean Pierre arrived first, with two friends, after a long flight from Paris. He could barely talk. He seemed to be having trouble holding his head up. I hugged him, but I didn't say anything. There was nothing to say.

Anne Marie's plane from Mexico City arrived some time later. The moment she spotted us, she burst into tears.

"I want to see her," she said. "I want to see my little girl."

We drove to the morgue. It was the last place in the world I wanted to be. Part of me still thought I was in the middle of a nightmare, an unusually vivid nightmare, to be sure, but I knew that I would soon wake up and life would go on as before.

I imagined Audrey, at my side, smiling. She was waving, diving, laughing, braiding her hair, making breakfast for Luca. She was outrunning me on the streets near our house, *our* house, and laughing at me. And there she was, reaching up to kiss the top of my bald head. Audrey Audrey Audrey.

But no. *That* was my imagination, working overtime. The reality was in front of us:

Audrey, being wheeled in on a cart, under a sheet. She looked like she was sleeping.

Oh, Jesus God.

Now, finally, I broke down in tears.

The next day went by in a blur. We packed up Audrey's things. Barely spoke. Shuffled around in a haze. Jean Pierre kept asking how this could have happened, and we kept apologizing, telling him we didn't know.

We want answers from life, but life doesn't often provide them. And when it does, they are seldom the answers we are looking for.

I remembered having asked myself on more than one occasion what I had done to deserve a woman like Audrey. Now I wondered what I had done to lose her.

The next day, the autopsy report came back, listing the official cause of death as accidental asphyxiation by immersion. In other words, drowning.

We flew back to Miami, taking Audrey's body with us, and a representative from the funeral home met us at the airport. We had made arrangements to have Audrey cremated, and we went to the funeral home for a brief ceremony. We played a song by Mylène Farmer, a Canadian singer who had a big following in France. Audrey was very fond of her. Mylène often sang about the afterlife.

We scattered Audrey's ashes at sea. We took the urn out on the *Olokun* to one of our old practice sites, three miles offshore. I had Anne Marie, Jean Pierre, Tata, Carlos, Wiky, Carolina, and Chelique on the boat, and three other boats followed close behind, loaded with Audrey's friends. It was an overcast day, and brutally hot. When we arrived at the site, I slipped into the water and Tata handed me the urn. It was my last dive with Audrey. I went ten meters down, opened the urn, and scattered her ashes. The particles hung in the water for a moment, refracting the light like a school of tiny fish.

Audrey and I had traveled the world together, and here I was, sending her off on her final journey. She was back in the place where life began. She was going home.

Audrey had always been happiest in the water, and it was in the water, together, that Audrey and I had found our greatest joy. I suddenly remembered Audrey playing with the whales in the Silver Bank, Audrey dwarfed by two fifty-ton creatures, and I recalled what she had said when she came up for air: "It was eerie. I almost felt as if they were calling to us."

Perhaps they had been calling to us. Or to her, anyway. If so, I hoped they were taking good care of her now.

Tata helped me out of the water. We stood there for a long while, not saying a word, feeling the boat rocking under our feet, dancing in the swells. I stared at the surface of the turquoise water, and I felt as if my life were over.

At that very moment, thousands of miles away, off the coast of Palavas, France, Audrey's family and friends were holding a memorial of their own. Pascal was there with them. He threw a dozen red roses into the sea.

Anne Marie and Jean Pierre stayed at the house with me for two more days. We were like ghosts, padding around, lost inside ourselves. Anne Marie helped me with the grim job of going through Audrey's things. She kept Audrey's favorite pen, a small bottle of perfume, a blouse, and a cookbook. I kept one of her dresses, her stuffed animals, her books and CDs, and her sketch pad. Everything else we put inside a big box, and early the next morning I found another, smaller box and went over to the corner of the living room where I kept my little offerings to Olokun. His candles. The ceramic bowl. The incense and the broken seashells. The smooth stones, polished by the sea. I put all of it into this smaller box, and I took both boxes out to the dock, and then I asked Anne Marie and Jean Pierre if they'd accompany me out to sea one more time.

We rode for hours, until there was no land in sight, and I dropped both boxes into the ocean. The ocean had taken Audrey, and I felt that it might as well take her things. As for the other box, that was for Olokun:

he hadn't protected Audrey, and I was done with him—and I wanted him to know it.

We watched both boxes bobbing in the water, then slowly sink out of sight. I turned to look at Anne Marie. She had tears in her eyes.

"I don't understand a God who can take away my little girl," she said, wiping her tears. "People keep telling me, 'It's God's will,' 'It's God's will,' but what kind of will is that? What kind of God does that to a person?"

When they left Miami, I returned to the empty house, to try to figure out how to get on with my life. But everywhere I looked, there she was. On the bed. In her drawings. In the scrapbooks she had assembled with such care. In the paintings on the wall. She was in the books and the photographs, and she was even in Noiraud, the stray cat she'd invited into our lives.

That first night, I sat in front of the computer and logged on to our website. There were hundreds and hundreds of tributes from people all over the world. Poland. Morocco. Jakarta. Most of the letters were from complete strangers, but from time to time a name I recognized would jump out at me.

"May our thoughts lighten your grief," Enzo Maiorca had written. "*Le grand bleu* has taken a beautiful woman."

At the end of the week, I found myself standing in front of a tattoo parlor in Miami Beach. I couldn't for the life of me remember how I'd gotten there, but I walked in with a drawing in my hand and set it down in front of the man behind the counter.

"Can you do that?" I said.

"Nice," the man said, taking the cigarette out of his mouth. "Very nice."

It was one of Audrey's drawings, the one of the mermaid pressed tight against the belly of a hammerhead. *Together Forever,* Audrey had written across the bottom. I no longer had Audrey, so I settled for the drawing. It is etched into the skin of my left calf. Forever, but not together.

In short order, very short order, the world must have felt that I'd had enough time to mourn, because suddenly the attacks began. On our website. In the newspapers. In magazines. People were looking for an explanation for Audrey's death. They wanted answers. But I didn't have any answers.

I didn't understand what it was they wanted to hear. That it was my fault? That I blamed myself? Of course I blamed myself. Audrey was *dead*. The woman I loved was gone. How could I *not* blame myself?

I'm the one who introduced her to the sport, remember? And maybe, just maybe, I had pushed her too hard. But I never pushed her too far. I never asked the impossible of Audrey. On the contrary, I always told her that the door was open, that she could walk away from anything, anytime; that if something didn't feel right, it wasn't right.

Were mistakes made? Yes. Absolutely.

We never double-checked the pony tank. We should have checked it with a gauge. But we had always worked together as a team, and that system, however haphazard it may have looked to other people, had always worked for us. Until then.

And why even argue this point? The computerized data is clear and unmistakable, and the video confirms it: the lift bag never fully inflated; there wasn't enough air in the tank to fill it.

Another point: we didn't have a diver at 120 meters. Should we have had a diver at 120 meters? Probably. I don't know. If I think about it now, I'd probably say yes, sure. But if we'd had a diver there, would Audrey be alive? I don't know. I can't answer that question. I doubt anyone can.

And what about Wiky? Why was he down there on compressed air, when he should have been on Trimix? Was that a mistake, too? Maybe. I'd even say probably. But that was never an issue. Wiky began his ascent because he thought the dive had been aborted. And he had good reason to think so: six minutes had elapsed. As Wiky himself pointed out, he assumed Audrey was below, buddy-breathing with Pascal, and that the two of them were slowly working their way up.

And think about it: even if he'd stayed and waited for them, they would have reached his side *six minutes* into the dive, at which point it was already too late.

As for Pascal, what could he have done differently? Audrey didn't ask for air. She didn't want to abort the dive. And we all knew Audrey: at one time or another, all of us had heard those five little words: "I can do it myself."

I was even criticized for not hiring a doctor, and for not having a defibrillator and an intubation kit on the boat. We had a medical team on board with vast experience in treating divers. Wasn't that enough?

In the weeks and months that followed, things got really ugly. People attacked me, and they attacked my crew. To them, the tragedy was ultimate proof of my cavalier attitude. I didn't care about safety. I did things any goddamn way I wanted. I was stubborn and irresponsible. Audrey was dead because she had put her trust in the wrong man.

They said my entire crew and my entire organization was criminally negligent. Not only should I have had more safety divers, but each one of them should have been equipped with an emergency lift bag. And why wasn't Audrey harnessed to the sled? If she had been, she wouldn't have fallen.

They criticized Pascal, too. They said Audrey was narked, and unable to think for herself, and that he should have forced her to take air as soon as things started going wrong. Then of course it occurred to them that taking air at that depth could have proved fatal, and they backed off—on this one charge, anyway.

But the stories only got stranger and more outlandish: I had done it on purpose. I wanted to stage a dramatic rescue at sea. Or, worse: I was too scared to go to that depth myself, so I had used Audrey as a guinea pig.

The attacks were truly beneath contempt. Didn't these people realize that I had lost the woman of my dreams; a woman I loved even more than my own life?

Am I responsible? Yes. In my heart and soul, I am responsible. It was my crew, and my organization. And no doubt mistakes were made. But I'm not sure that anyone else could have done any better. Not with more divers. Not with more rules and regulations. Not with a goddamn floating hospital waiting on the surface.

This is the life we chose, or the life that chose us. Skydiver, tightrope walker, slalom skier, mountaineer. It's all about risk, about living on the edge. For Audrey and me, life was an adventure, and No Limits was a big part of that adventure.

Audrey believed that she was immortal. She didn't doubt it for a second. Blood, flesh, bone—to her, it was a vessel; something to be discarded when the journey was over. This is what Audrey believed: that the light that shines inside each of us finds a new home when the time comes. And I wish I believed that, too. Part of me wants desperately to believe it, especially now, with Audrey gone. I'd like to think that we all have many lives, and that Audrey has just moved on, that's she's fine, happy even. But I don't know. It's a little too esoteric for me. Maybe death is nothing more than death. It just ends. There's nothing else out there. And it means nothing. You had your time on earth and now it's over and there's absolutely nothing else.

But not Audrey. Audrey had no doubts whatsoever. Audrey was sure she was going to take that light with her and travel to another place.

"How can you *not* believe?" she used to tell me. "To laugh and swim and breathe and feel and hear and touch and love—that in and of itself is a miracle."

For many months, I sank into a deep depression. I couldn't eat. I took pills to get to sleep. I lost twenty pounds. I ignored the business until there was no business left. Carlos split, hoping to find work elsewhere. Carolina hung on, trying to figure out what she could do for me.

One day I remembered my old hero, Jacques Mayol, the lover of dolphins, and I thought about the brief time we spent together at his villa, in Elba. Two years earlier, at that very villa, Mayol had tied a rope around his neck and hung himself. I didn't know enough about the circumstances of his death to understand what had driven him to take his life, but I certainly understood the feeling.

At night, I would sit on my dock, crying. Even if everything Audrey believed was real, what good did it do me? She wasn't there. And I missed her. I was falling apart. I didn't care about anything anymore. I didn't have the strength to go in to the office. I hadn't gone diving in months. I couldn't bring myself to go in the water.

My mother called from Cuba, trying to comfort me. "Audrey was madly in love with you," she said. "All these things you feel—the sadness, the anger, the guilt—she wouldn't have wanted you to let them destroy you."

Tata called. He'd been plagued by insomnia since Audrey's death. "She was the Michael Jordan of free diving," he said. "She was the best there is."

"I know," I said.

Pascal phoned from France from time to time. In the course of his career, he had recovered the bodies of half a dozen divers, including that of Cédric Darolles, one of his closest friends. But Audrey's death had affected him so deeply that he felt he would never shake it. "I keep asking myself what I could have done differently," he said.

"Nothing," I said. "Nothing."

"I wouldn't have been down there if I'd had any doubts, you know," he added. "But I didn't have any doubts because Audrey didn't have any doubts. She went into it with all her heart."

Yes, I thought. *And now she was gone, leaving a mass of broken hearts in her wake.*

Anne Marie phoned. In some ways, on some level, I'm sure she felt I had taken her daughter from her, but here she was, the bereaved mother, calling to cheer me up, calling to give me hope.

"You know," she said, "the seven years Audrey spent with you were the best years of her life."

I couldn't answer. I was fighting tears.

"I know you haven't gone back to the sea," she continued. "But maybe that's a mistake. Maybe when you're down there, doing what you love best, Audrey will somehow let you know she's thinking of you."

A few days later, I took the *Olokun* out to sea. I drove through Government Cut, past the cruise ships and the freighters, past Fisher Island and the tip of South Beach, and on out, to Fowey Light, where Audrey and I had passed so many pleasant hours together. I cut the motor and let the current nudge the boat, then reached for my fins, mask, and snorkel, and jumped into the water.

It was another unusually hot day, even for Miami, and the moment I hit the water, something happened. Something *electric*. The water felt *alive* against my skin.

Oh, I know what you're thinking. I know. You're thinking it was nothing at all. That it was just me, wanting to believe, desperate to make contact. But I think you're wrong. I know what I felt. I felt Audrey in the water with me. Suddenly I knew that I wasn't alone and that I'd never be alone again.

Audrey wasn't really gone. She was down there, waiting for me. And she'd be there every time I went into the water.

↓

Chapter_ TEN:

A TRIBUTE

Cozumel, January 2000: Moments before taking the plunge.

I returned home from Fowey Light feeling transformed. It was time to get back in the water, and I intended to do it right: I was going to make a dive in Audrey's memory. I would do it on our wedding day, August 18, and I would travel to a depth of 170 meters, to commemorate her final dive.

As soon as the story hit the papers, the phone calls began. Old friends, former enemies, members of my crew, reporters. Just about everyone I heard from was wildly supportive and glad to see me back on my feet. They were rooting for me, they said. Diving was my life, and it was high time I took it back.

One of the reporters who called was a man called Gary Smith. He came to see me and wrote a story for *Sports Illustrated* that ended up on the June 16, 2003, cover: "The Deadly Dive: Love and Obsession 500 Feet Down in the Dangerous Quest for the World Record." For some reason I still can't fathom, the magazine included a photograph of Audrey, laid out on a stretcher after the accident. As a result, I couldn't bring myself to read the piece, and I never have.

On the west coast of the country, however, in Los Angeles, film director Jim Cameron read the story and immediately got in touch. He flew down to Miami to meet me, and we spent hours talking and looking at videotape and discussing the appeal of the sport. Cameron is a committed diver, with more than a passing interest in the sea. He was responsible for *Titanic,* one of the most successful films in motion picture history, and for *The Abyss,* which contained one of the most emotionally harrowing underwater sequences I have ever seen.

"If you really want to understand this sport," I told him. "You need to see it for yourself."

I told him I was planning a tribute dive in August, right there in Miami, and I invited him to become part of it. Unfortunately, Cameron was not going to be available in August, so we discussed the possibility of moving it forward to October 12, the anniversary of Audrey's death. And he didn't want me to make the dive in Miami. He was hoping I could meet him in Cabo San Lucas, which was so much closer to his crew in Los Angeles, and to his equipment—which included his own personal submarine.

I was reluctant at first. I had met Audrey in Cabo, and I didn't want to stir up all those memories, but I agreed to do it. Maybe it would turn out to be a pleasant experience. Maybe it would turn out to be cathartic.

"This is just the beginning," Cameron told me. "I'm going to take your story—this incredible love story, Audrey and you—and I'm going to turn it into a movie."

In the weeks and months ahead, I concentrated on getting my forty-two-year-old body back in shape. I hit the weights every day, I jogged around the neighborhood, and I was in the water, practicing, at least three times a week.

As the summer drew to a close, I knew it was time to put the team together, and I picked up the phone and began making calls to all corners of the world. It had been almost ten months since Audrey's death, and none of us had had much contact, and now I understood why. Just the sound of my voice brought it all back, and it was enough to reduce most of us to tears.

Some of the crew committed on the spot. Pascal said he would be there, and Tata assured me I could count on him: "Just name the day, *brodel.*" And Kim McCoy had reservations, but he signed on.

Others, like Matt Briseno, couldn't handle it. Matt had been on the boat with us on that fateful day, trying desperately to revive Audrey, and he was still having a hard time with it. "I'm finished with this, man," he said. "I don't want to be there when it happens to you."

I invited Wiky, too, but he never returned any of my calls.

And I called Carlos, who had finally moved on, worn down by all those endless battles over safety precautions, with AIDA and with me, but who had always treated me like a brother, who remained a true friend even after the partnership fell apart.

"I need you, man," I said. "I trust you. You're the one who can make it happen."

Carlos looked at me and smiled. He was onboard.

Tata, Carlos, Pascal, Kim. Four members of the original team. I would have liked to think they were doing it for me, but I knew better. They were doing it for themselves. They needed closure as much as I did.

We arrived in Cabo San Lucas a good ten days before Jim Cameron, wanting to get settled and organized and do a few practice dives before the big day. It was a strange reunion, four people who had been damaged by a terrible tragedy, together again in this place so filled with memories.

The other recruits included Gido Braase, a German-born videographer from Boston who specialized in extreme sports; Eric "The Kid" Doucette, an experienced diver from Maine; Chris Brandson, of Grand Cayman, an accomplished underwater photographer; and Hubert Foucart, a computer engineer from France who had been brought along by Pascal, his cave-diving buddy.

Cabo had become wildly overdeveloped since I'd last visited. It was crawling with tourists, from carefree students to pale, Midwestern Hemingway-wannabes, and they were all there for the same reason we were there: love of the water.

Unfortunately, Hurricane Marty slammed into the peninsula shortly after we arrived, and we were left without electricity for five days. With no air-conditioning, the rooms were sweltering, so I took to walking around town, braving the flooded streets and trying hard not to think of Audrey.

It wasn't easy. Everywhere I looked, there she was. In Margaritavilla, the bar where we first met. On the beach, where we took our first,

Audrey in the Cayman Islands. She fell in love with the water before she could walk.

moonlight walk. At her hotel, that night she sent me on my way, near dawn, then had a sudden change of heart and called me back.

I began to feel crushingly depressed. And walking along the streets didn't help. Half the town was flooded, the sewers were backed up, and everywhere I turned I ran into noisy work crews, trying to restore order.

My mood grew darker. I avoided the others. I was hostile and uncommunicative, and told them I wanted to be left alone. I was suffering, and my pain was manifesting itself in ugly ways.

The only time I found a modicum of peace was when I jumped into the ocean. Then the old feeling would come back: *Here I am, where I belong.*

On the sixth day, the power was restored, and Carlos got to work, bringing order to chaos. He drew up a schedule, pulled together all the equipment we needed, hired a team of paramedics, and discussed an emergency plan with the hospital staff that ran the hyperbaric chamber—which struck me as a little much. He also found two more safety divers right there in town, which I thought was completely unnecessary.

I had hoped that Carlos and I would bridge the distance that had come to separate us after Audrey's death, but it didn't happen. We had never really been able to discuss the tragedy, and we remained unable to do so. Many months earlier, Carlos had asked me to sit with him and look at a video of the accident, captured by the sled-mounted camera, but I was unable to do so, and I haven't looked at it to this day. He hadn't asked me to look at it because he wanted to torture me, but because he thought that, together, we might be able to figure out exactly what went wrong. I wanted no part of it, however. I wanted to deal with the past by not dealing with it.

Of course, now that we were in Cabo, preparing this tribute, it was hard to avoid. We found ourselves dealing with Audrey's death all over again.

Carlos dealt with it by putting a four-man medical team on the dive barge, which led to our first blowup. I showed up for our first practice dive, found the team waiting, and promptly turned around and went back to the hotel. I have never been crazy about doctors, and Carlos knew it, and I found their presence horribly unnerving.

"If you don't get rid of them, I'm not diving," I said.

"We need them there," he said. "The whole world will be watching this dive, and we need to do it right."

I didn't give a damn. I thought it was overkill. There were too many medical people, and too many safety divers, and too much bullshit. "I don't want all these emergency people on the boat, and I sure as hell don't want more people in the water," I said. "That's where we always run into problems. With the safety divers."

"We're going to have to figure this out, Pipín," Carlos said, barely contained. "I didn't come here to watch you die."

In the end, Carlos didn't watch me at all. It was clear we were never going to resolve our differences, neither the ones on the surface nor those buried deep within, and he was on the next plane back to Miami.

On Sunday, October 5, without Carlos, we did our first practice dive. Before we had even started, the anchor fell off an undersea shelf and dragged the line down after it, almost taking me with it. After I got done screaming at everyone for their incompetence—"¡Anormales!"—I did a shaky, 130-meter dive. Here, again, we had a problem—but this time largely of my own making. I had asked Tata to put a clamp on the line at precisely forty feet from the surface. I was worried about crashing into the barge, or worse, because the current was strong and the line was drifting badly, but I didn't realize how violently the line would jerk when I hit it with the sled. This put both Pascal and Hubert in danger. They were far below, in pitch-darkness, clinging to the line, and when I hit the clamp they almost lost their grip—their literal lifeline to the surface.

Worse still, the dive itself hadn't gone well. I'd only been under for two minutes, but when I surfaced my lips had begun to turn blue. This meant I was dangerously close to blacking out. "I'm worried about you, *socio,*" Tata said. "Why don't we forget about one seventy? I know the Hollywood guys are coming, but so what? One twenty-five is a good dive, too."

"No," I said. "I'm doing this for Audrey. If I don't do one seventy, it's meaningless."

"To whom?"

"To me," I said.

By the time Cameron and his crew arrived, with two camera-equipped minisubs, I was ready. I was a little shaky, admittedly, but I was ready. The point of Cameron's trip was to get a handle on the logistics of No Limits free diving. He wanted to know exactly what it looked like, and how he was going to make it play on the big screen. Salma Hayek, the actress, was interested in the role of Audrey, and she had come to Cabo with Jim and his crew, which included the two people who ran his company, Rae Sanchini and John Landau.

On that first day, Cameron set up a staging area for his two subs in a vacant lot that backed up to the docks. Watching this felt a little strange. Our bare-bones tribute was becoming a major Hollywood production.

On Tuesday, with Cameron and his crew in position, I did another practice dive, hoping to reach 155 meters. The subs were lowered by crane into the water, then towed out to the dive site and maneuvered into position. When they were finally in place, I took that last gasping breath and pulled the cord and plunged in. But less than twenty seconds into the trip I hit something and was forced to abort the dive. I thought I had struck one of my safety divers, or one of the cameramen, but it turned out that the decompression line had drifted into my own line, carried up against it by the strong current.

On Wednesday, we tried again, and I aimed a little deeper: 160 meters. We didn't have that many dress rehearsals left, and I needed to get as close as possible to my target. We got a late start, though, and the wind wreaked havoc with the dive barge. We had to tow it back out to sea, but we were still too close to the undersea wall. Instead of canceling the dive, however, I opted to trim a few meters from my goal. I plunged in and hit 135 meters and rocketed back to the surface in 2 minutes and 25 seconds. For some reason, one of my ears was bleeding a little, and the medical technicians moved in to check me out. I really didn't want them there, but I didn't want to make a fuss in front of all those people, especially since they seemed so happy. Cameron and his crew felt they had managed to get some spectacular footage of the dive, and they were walking on air.

That night, back in my hotel room, the phone rang—and it kept right on ringing. Friends were calling from Miami to tell me that Carlos and Wiky had given an interview to Telemundo, the Spanish-language network in Miami. Not only were they badmouthing me and the tribute dive, but they wanted to rehash Audrey's death and all the mistakes that had been made. To hear Carlos tell it—*Carlos,* my friend, a man who had been like a brother to me—Audrey would be alive today if not for Pipín Ferreras.

I realized that the dive was opening old wounds, but I wasn't going to stand for these ugly, baseless accusations. Outraged, and shaking with anger, I went over to my laptop and wrote a long, rambling, virulent response, which I posted on my website. In retrospect, I know it was a mistake. I had let my emotions get the better of me, and it was not a pretty sight.

When I was done, as the sun was coming up, I was still shaking, but I was no longer angry. I felt I was done with more than the letter. I was finally done with all this *inmundicia,* all this bullshit. Nobody seemed to understand that I missed Audrey more than all the rest of them put together, and that I would miss her every day for the rest of my life. And since they would never understand, there was no point in fighting them. I was going to move on with my life. After all, that's why I was in Cabo.

On Friday, October 10, we set the line for another practice dive. This time I would try for 163 meters, one more than my own personal best. It was a huge test of my will. Thirty-three months had passed since that 162-meter dive in Cozumel, and I hadn't forgotten the blackouts. I was filled with self-doubt. I wasn't a young man anymore. Was it over for me? Was I finished?

Kim added 24 pounds to the sled to speed up the rate of descent. At my previous speed, a 170-meter dive would have taken 3 minutes and 20 seconds, and I knew I could have handled it, but Kim wanted to err on the side of caution.

Fortunately, my fears and concerns were somewhat allayed by the good weather. There wasn't much wind, either, and with the help of Cameron's crew we threw another anchor into the water and easily stabilized the barge.

At 11:45 A.M., I began to ventilate, then I did a series of short, warm-up dives. Cameron was in the sub at the bottom of the line, almost in position, but suddenly he radioed up to say that he needed another minute: huge packs of shrimplike krill were swarming around his sub, attracted by the light, and they were obstructing the cameras.

I did another warm-up, feeling a little off, a little unsteady. This time I went about thirty meters down the line, and suddenly something clicked. I felt that same electric energy I'd felt that day at Fowey Light. The water seemed *alive.*

I returned to the surface, energized. Cameron was back in position. The countdown began.

I felt my confidence returning. Tata grabbed the release cord. Everyone watched in silence. I took one final breath and Tata pulled the cord and I shot down the line like a bullet. A third of the way down, I almost abandoned the sled, but I forced myself to keep going. I reached the bottom in one minute and 25 seconds, and felt so unbelievably pumped that I opened my eyes to make sure I wasn't dreaming. I saw the blazing lights of Cameron's sub and smiled and waved in his direction, then I turned my attention to the lift bag, and—boom!—I was flying toward the surface. I was grinning ear to ear when I broke through, and everyone was cheering. I felt goddamn unstoppable.

When I got on the boat, Kim's computer told us I'd fallen one meter shy of my personal record. But 161 meters was still pretty damn good. I wasn't going to complain. I was *back*. I only needed another nine meters to hit my mark. Saturday was a day of rest, but Sunday—Sunday was Audrey's day.

* * *

On the big day, just before we went out to the site, I took Tata aside. "If anything goes wrong," I said. "If I'm unconscious, if it doesn't look like I'm coming back, I want you to tie a weight belt around my waist and let me go."

"Don't ask me to do that, *brodel,*" he said. "I don't even want you to *think* like that."

"I know," I said. "But I need your promise."

Tata nodded his head, but none too happily.

It was an exceptionally beautiful day. The sea was calm and the sky was a crisp, cerulean blue. We rode out to the platform on a small launch and I greeted the crew with few words. Everyone was quiet, contained. This was Audrey's day and they all knew it.

The crew checked and double-checked everything. They were calm, efficient, professional, and they were also nervous. The last thing they wanted, on the anniversary of Audrey's death, was another death.

The time was drawing near. We got ready. Pascal would be at 170 meters, Hubert at 120, Chris at 70, Eric at 30, and Gido at 20. Tata would remain on the surface.

Kim added another 10 pounds to the sled, bringing the total to 135 pounds. I had never used that much weight, but I needed to get there fast. I was going to cover two meters per second on the descent, and twice that on the ascent. The plan was to make the entire trip in less than three minutes.

At 10:30 A.M., I got in the water with Tata.

On the shoulder of my bright green wet suit, I had written *"En Tu Memoria, Audrey."* In your memory, Audrey.

A dozen spectator boats assembled downwind from the platform, including a big party yacht. I looked out toward Land's End, some three hundred yards away, and felt oddly peaceful.

I did three short warm-up dives, then nodded at Kim to let him know I was ready. At precisely 11:25 A.M., he began the countdown.

Pascal, Hubert, Chris, Eric, and Gido slipped below the surface.

Tata came over to strap the depth computer to my back.

"*¿Todo bien, socio?*" he asked.

I nodded. All was well. Never better.

I knelt on the sled and wrapped my hands around the pole. I kept breathing. Exhale, inhale. Exhale, inhale. I was packing my body with air. I was irrigating my blood and organs with pure, life-sustaining oxygen.

"Zero minutes," Kim said.

It was time to go. I took two more gulping breaths and nodded. Tata yanked the green cord, and I was on my way.

The sled shot down the line, singing its metallic song. I could hear my heart now, beating in my ears, strong, confident.

Then—a clanking noise. I had just passed Hubert. I had another 50 meters to go, a long way, certainly, but I felt I could keep going forever.

Then, whoosh! Before I knew it, I had reached the bottom. I was 170 meters down. Only one other person had ever reached that depth, and it was Audrey. God, how I missed her!

I disconnected the sled and felt for the valve above my head, just below the lift bag. And suddenly I was overwhelmed with the desire to *not* go back. It would be so easy. All I had to do was stay.

What was it Audrey had said? *Sometimes it's a real drag coming back up.*

With my hand still hovering over the valve, I opened my eyes, and God help me: there she was. Audrey. Audrey transformed. Audrey as light and energy, glowing and translucent and vividly *alive.*

"Audrey?"

She drifted toward me, until our faces were almost touching.

"Is it you?"

She smiled, and I could feel her hand on my hand. Warm, insistent.

"Audrey?"

Then I felt my fingers on the valve and the lift bag popped open and I was suddenly gone, rocketing toward home.

I heard the roars when I broke through the surface, and as my eyes adjusted to the light I could make out the mad, colorful swirl of bodies on the surrounding boats. They were all cheering, dancing, clapping, blowing kisses, but all I heard was *Audrey Audrey Audrey.*

Oh, Audrey. My beautiful Audrey. My little water goddess.

"The sea is where we found each other," Audrey used to say. "And more than any other place, it is our home."

Yes, Audrey. More than any other place, the sea is our home.

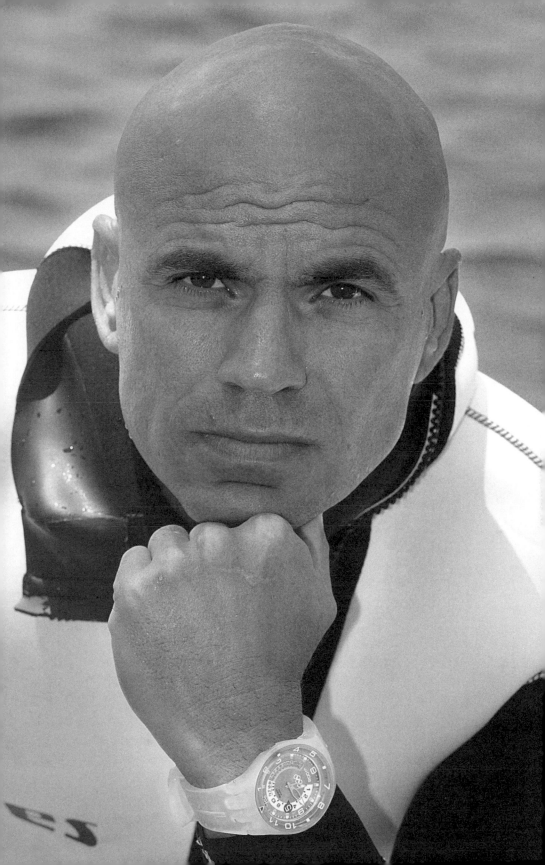